THE LORD'S PRAYER FOR TODAY

THE LORD'S PRAYER FOR TODAY

William J. Carl III

Westminster John Knox Press
LOUISVILLE • LONDON

Book design by Sharon Adams
Cover design by Eric Walljasper, Minneapolis, MN

First edition
Published by Westminster John Knox Press
Louisville, Kentucky

This book is printed on acid-free paper that meets the American National Standards Institute Z39.48 standard. ∞

PRINTED IN THE UNITED STATES OF AMERICA

06 07 08 09 10 11 12 13 14 15—10 9 8 7 6 5 4 3 2 1

Library of Congress Cataloging-in-Publication Data is on file at the Library of Congress, Washington, D.C.

ISBN-13: 978-0-664-22957-3
ISBN-10: 0-664-22957-3

Dedicated to

Gil and Billie Thomas,
Dan and Dorothy Foster,
John and Nancy Anderson

True mentors in my faith

Contents

Series Introduction

*T*he For Today series is intended to provide reliable and accessible resources for the study of important biblical texts, theological documents, and Christian practices. The series is written by experts who are committed to making the results of their studies available to those with no particular biblical or theological training. The goal is to provide an engaging means to study texts and practices that are familiar to laity in churches. The authors are all committed to the importance of their topics and to communicating the significance of their understandings to a wide audience. The emphasis is not only on what these subjects have meant in the past, but also on their value in the present—"For Today."

Our hope is that the books in this series will find eager readers in churches, particularly in the context of education classes. The authors are educators and pastors who wish to engage church laity in the issues raised by their topics. They seek to provide guidance for learning, for nurture, and for growth in Christian experience.

To enhance the educational usefulness of these volumes, Questions for Discussion are included at the end of each chapter.

We hope the books in this series will be important resources to enhance Christian faith and life.

The Publisher

1

Pray Then like This . . .

Οὕτως οὖν προσεύχεσθε ὑμεῖς

ΟΥΤШC ΟΥΝ ΠΡΟCΕΥΧΕCΘΕ ΥΜΕΙC

Why another book on the Lord's Prayer? There are hundreds out there already. My answer is threefold. First, from childhood I have had a lifelong love affair with this great prayer. Second, the universal impact the Jesus prayer has had and continues to have liturgically, theologically, and devotionally on the life of the church transcends that of any other document of comparable length. Third, the "Our Father" is acutely attuned to the needs of the twenty-first century.

I begin with my almost childlike fascination with this ancient prayer. You'd think a youngster wouldn't waste time on something so old from such an old book. Children want the newest and the latest, whatever it is. But the simplicity of this deep and profound prayer draws us in at the most basic levels of communication, no matter how young or old we are. Try as we may, there is no way to conjure up a new and improved version of it. We don't need James Fowler or Robert Coles to tell us; we know it intuitively—children seem to have an innate, precognitive sense of spirituality that elicits a kind of magnetic pull into the mystical and the holy. Children talk to God naturally, directly. Their brave and honest prayer is disarmingly fresh in its candid expression, as with the boy who prayed one night, "Dear God, thanks for the little sister, but I asked for a puppy." The next night he prayed, "Lord, if you can't make me a better boy, don't worry about it. I'm having a real good time just the way I am!"

We chuckle at children's frankness and their conversational relationship with the Almighty, an easy rapport that we as adults covet. For some of us it seems as if God has become a long-lost friend, the friend we once had. We just haven't kept in touch. We see the Gideon Bible in the motel room, but the pages don't come alive anymore. We hear the children sing, "Jesus loves me, this I know," and wonder why we don't believe it, why we don't feel it anymore. It all began when we stopped talking.

Children teach us how to talk to God. But they also need a little instruction along the way, otherwise they never grow up in the faith. Thus, responsible parents and teachers do their best to teach their children spiritually as a way of helping shape and encourage their pilgrimage in the faith. We mentor them with grace before meals and nighttime prayers. In our family we said one with our boys when they were growing up that was a more positive variation of the prayer-poem we've all heard:

> Now I lay me down to sleep;
> I pray the Lord my soul to keep.
> *Glad and well may I awake;*
> *This I pray for Jesus' sake.*

It's actually a modern version of Jesus' "Into thy hands I commit my spirit," from Psalm 31, as he gives himself finally and completely over to God at the end, like a child falling asleep in a parent's arms at the end of the day.

Notice the positive third line in the poem that replaces "If I should die before I wake," a phrase that has struck terror in many a child's heart and soul. Prayer shouldn't "scare the hell" out of children. It should introduce them to the joys of heaven and the possibilities "on earth as [they are] in heaven." That's exactly what the Lord's Prayer does. It encourages an affirmative view of God and our participation as believers in God's activity on earth. Like "Now I lay me down to sleep," the Lord's Prayer works as a great nighttime prayer, one that many parents teach their children to say from memory at a very early age. I don't recall exactly when I began saying this endearing prayer, but it was so early in my life that it is embedded in my spiritual consciousness and has helped shape my devotional psyche throughout my life.

With their facile linguistic agility, children can memorize this famous prayer in no time. When I taught New Testament Greek at Union Theological Seminary in Virginia, I would often bring our sons into class the first day, when they were three, four, and five years of age, stand them up on a desk, and say, "Go," then watch seventy or eighty surprised seminary students listen to the toddlers recite the Lord's Prayer in Greek. After an appropriately pregnant pause, I would say, "Now, if they can say it at their age, think how fast you can learn it." Talk about getting a whole Greek class's attention! Such is the occasional trauma for PKs, in this case, "professor's kids." So far as I know, this early recitation stunted neither Jeremy's nor David's growth. Years later, I taught this same ancient prayer to small children in Guguletu, a black township outside Cape Town, South Africa. I was stunned at how quickly they learned it, and then remembered that they had already made the switch from Xhosa to English, and Greek was easy after that.

The rhythm and timbre of this prayer when reciting it aloud in Greek are truly poetic and powerful. Perhaps that's what children love—the sheer beauty of its musical cadence as it is being spoken with a bit of a lilt in one's voice. In other words, the Lord's Prayer carries believers, especially young ones, into a transcendent place through a liturgical, hymnic quality that enhances the theological content even before we understand it all. Thus belonging leads to belief, which influences behavior and gives credence to Calvin's idea of prevenient grace. Long before we comprehend any of it intellectually we are experiencing it all emotionally at very early periods in our life. The same is true as we age, when it comes to the Jesus Prayer. Years after those Greek classes, I find that the Lord's Prayer is practically all that those students can recall (unless they went on and completed a PhD in New Testament studies), and many to this day can still recite the whole thing from memory because we said it as the opening prayer in class every day.

Once while preaching at the United Reformed Church in Cambridge, England, I told a story about a former student who had recited perfectly the entire prayer in Greek in answer to an examination question for ordination at a large presbytery meeting. As part of the story I also recited the Greek version of the prayer in its entirety. After the worship service one of the church members told my host that over half of the parishioners were saying it under their breath with me. Now that's an educated congregation! After all, most of them were fellows, tutors, and students at the various colleges of Cambridge University. Some of them were retired professors who had obviously learned the Lord's Prayer in Greek at an early age.

That's the thing about the Lord's Prayer—it sticks with you from childhood to old age. It lifts you up when all you seem to be is down. It carries you to places you have never been before. In other words, it stands the test of time. That has certainly been the case for two thousand years, a span of time that dwarfs our tiny lives. Imagine the power of this single, little prayer to transform whole nations and cultures. Why? Because of its sheer universality. On a shelf in my study is a book titled *On Earth as It Is in Heaven: The Lord's Prayer in Forty Languages*.[1] One immediately sees in this volume the staying power of this global prayer. Of course, forty versions of it represent only the tip of the iceberg; there are thousands, as many as there are languages, both extant and extinct.

Why are so many people from so many cultures drawn to this prayer? I believe it's because it speaks to the most common denominator in the human species—the soul. By that I mean the Hebrew understanding of soul (נֶפֶשׁ, *nephesh*) more than the Greek one (ψυχή, *psyche*). The Hebrew idea takes in all of who we are, because *nephesh* equals life principle, living being, appetite and emotion, volition, body and soul; in other words, the whole self and person, not the Greek immortal soul. Each individual is a *nephesh*. You don't have a soul, you are a soul, which includes the totality of who you are—mind, body, emotions, faith, trust, moral behavior. *Nephesh* literally means "throat," which intakes food and breath, so the *nephesh* hungers, thirsts, grieves, loves, and hopes. Thus it is the true nature of *nephesh* to know its own limitations and long for more—something and someone it cannot get on its own, and something deeper and more fulfilling than the world can ever give. Something we cannot buy.

Enter the Lord's Prayer, stage left.

Everett Fullam rightly notes that Jesus wasn't setting forth another liturgical incantation. "He was setting forth a way of life." Thus, "To understand the Lord's Prayer and to pray it in absolute sincerity is to embrace a whole concept of being. It addresses every aspect of life."[2] It demands our lives, our souls, our all. No wonder Tertullian calls the Lord's Prayer "a brief summary of the whole gospel."[3]

Perhaps that's what the disciples realized. They had tried to pray with all their might, even in the Garden of Gethsemane. But the true and holy one, this Jesus, could pray them all under the table, even the Lord's Table at the Last Supper. He would go off on spiritual marathons, praying and fasting for days on end. Instead of returning cranky and weak from hunger, he seemed refreshed and fulfilled. The disciples took one look at him and said to themselves, "Whatever he's got, I want some of it." So, they asked him one day, "Teach us to pray," and instead of launching into a six-week Lenten seminar on "The Power of Prayer for Today's Living," he simply said, "Pray then like this . . . ," and off he went.

I wonder if they were amazed when they heard it, or if they even comprehended the depth and profundity of these few simple phrases. They say that people weren't impressed the day Lincoln delivered his little Gettysburg Address. On the contrary, everyone marveled at Edward Everett Hale's eloquent two-hour oration that day. But which one has stood the test of time? Chances are the disciples didn't "get" the true import of what Jesus was laying out before them at first; after all, they rarely caught on to much of anything he said. He always had to stop and explain things to them. But even if they didn't catch every nuance of this deep prayer, there must have been a hush when he finished as they pondered the significance of his words. Some of it must have had traction in their liturgical life, or else the prayer would never have survived.

As we enter a century shaken by 9/11 terrorism, wars and rumors of wars, tsunamis and hurricanes, this little prayer continues to speak and "make sense" in our time. With postmodern, post-Christendom secularism on the one hand and radical fundamentalism and runaway global evangelism that sometimes ignores social justice on the other, the Jesus prayer patterns for us a way to avoid both narrow sectarianism and patriotic triumphalism. It lifts us beyond a saccharine "me and Jesus" religion that threatens to turn us in on ourselves in narcissistic navel gazing, the worst sort of hell one could ever imagine. It saves us from ourselves if we truly listen to it and heed its advice.

In the twenty-first century the Lord's Prayer, especially its second set of petitions, reminds us in a truly incarnational way of our responsibility for the world, the environment, and those who are helpless. Daniel Migliore puts it this way: "When spoken from the depths of our own need and in solidarity with the poor of the earth whose voices have long been silent, the Lord's Prayer proves to be a profoundly liberating prayer. Called to prayer, we are summoned not to passivity but to activity, . . . not to indifference about evil in and around us but to passion for justice, freedom and peace in the whole creation."[4]

Through this model prayer, Jesus nudges us in the direction of true and abundant life, which is the natural response to the experience of salvation. There is risk here, though. If we open ourselves to all that this prayer means, we are inviting God into our lives to do some serious renovation. Through this prayer God enters the houses of our existential lives and begins knocking down walls and rearranging things, and that's almost always painful. In the end, of course, it leads to peace and healing, the true meaning of salvation. Σωτηρία (*soteria*), the Greek word for salvation, has a much more holistic connotation than narrow exegetes would ever want to admit. It means wholeness, peace, and healing for all of who you are, for the whole community and indeed the whole creation. In many ways *soteria* is a synonym for *shālōm* in Hebrew and *salām* in Arabic. "Peace be with you, and also with you," is another way of saying that, because God loves me, I care for you and for the whole world.

The Lord's Prayer teaches a more resonant responsibility from its first petition to its last. But readers beware. You cannot understand this prayer's deeper meaning without being changed, metamorphosed. If you are not ready for that, you should put this book back on the shelf in your church library or take it to the bookstore for a refund, because change from top to bottom is what Jesus is after with this little prayer. In other words, it packs a wallop. If you are ready and open to alteration in your ways of thinking and acting, then fasten your seatbelt. You are in for the ride of a lifetime.

Questions for Discussion

1. Can you remember when you first said the Lord's Prayer? Recount your earliest recollections of saying it and how you felt about it as a child.
2. How has your understanding of the Lord's Prayer changed through the years?

3. What traumatic events in your life that left you feeling helpless brought you back to the Lord's Prayer and gave you a greater appreciation for its ability to speak to all sorts of conditions, predicaments, and situations in life? In other words, how has the Lord's Prayer centered you and given you a greater sense of peace?
4. How has the Lord's Prayer helped you be a better Christian, spouse, friend, parent, coworker, and citizen?

2

Our Father Who Art in Heaven

Πάτερ ἡμῶν ὁ ἐν τοῖς οὐρανοῖς

ΠΔΤΕΡ ΗΜШΝ Ο ΕΝ ΤΟΙϹ ΟΥΡΔΝΟΙϹ

*H*ave you noticed that practically everyone prays at one time or another? Some complain about there being no prayer in schools. But there's plenty of prayer in schools right before every exam! We all pray at one time or another. Even atheists pray in foxholes, and also in doctor's offices when they hear the dreaded cancer word. "What can it hurt?" they say to themselves with a lump in their throats. Prayer is something you do when you're in trouble, and sooner or later we all get into trouble. Just about the time you think things are going along beautifully, something happens to cure that feeling. Before you know it you're back on your knees and back in church looking for some help, because you finally realize you've exhausted all your human resources and there's nowhere else to turn. Some people offer prayers the way sailors use pumps—only when the ship leaks. But the point is, whether out of desperation or frustration, sooner or later we all find ourselves talking to God.

Which is probably the reason Jesus says, "And when you pray," not if, but when, "when you happen to pray, here's the way to do it. Don't show off. Keep it brief and to the point." Eugene Peterson gives us the context for this simple advice by suggesting that the world is not a stage where God is the audience when he translates Jesus' words in Matthew 6 this way. "When you are trying to be good don't make a performance out of it. It might be good theater but the God who made you is not applauding. When you do something for someone else, don't call attention to yourself . . . treating prayer meetings and street corners alike as a stage, acting compassionate as long as someone is watching, playing to the crowds. . . . When you help someone out, don't think about how it looks. Just do it—quietly and unobtrusively. That is the way your God, who conceived you in love, working behind the scenes, helps you out. And when you come before God, don't turn that into a theatrical production either. All these people making a regular show out of their prayers, hoping for stardom! Do you think God sits in a box seat? . . . The world is full of so-called prayer warriors who are prayer-ignorant. They're full of formulas ,and programs, peddling techniques for getting what you want from God. Don't fall for that nonsense. This is your Father you are dealing with, and he knows better than you what you need. With a God like this loving you, you can pray very simply."[1] Like this: "Our Father who art in heaven . . ." And off he goes with one of the shortest, most profound prayers in human history. It's the God prayer and the people's prayer. Some believe it's a misnomer to call it the Lord's Prayer, since the Lord would never pray it, because the ones who pray it ask for forgiveness, and Jesus would never do that. But in many ways it is the Lord's Prayer because it is the Lord who said it and who has given it to us. Some people call it the "Our Father," or the *Pater Noster*. Whatever you want to call it, it changes your life if you pray it daily and allow its deep meaning to soak through and saturate your soul. Emmet Fox calls it the Great Prayer, and describes it as a "compact formula for the development of the soul."[2]

Mountaintop experiences alone will not change your soul—that is, the essence of your being, that inner life that is visible to the world through your words and your deeds. Don't get me wrong—mountaintop experiences are great, but are often difficult to interpret and usually yield only a temporary high. Then it's back to the day-to-day routine, where we so easily forget about God, even those of us who busy ourselves daily with "church work." Great lectures can fill your mind with new ideas, but even stirring intellect in the end cannot by itself change your soul.

The only thing that will truly alter who you are existentially and make you a better person, more at peace with yourself and others, able to do more than you've ever done before, is the daily practice of prayer, especially praying the prayer Jesus gave his disciples. "When you pray, . . . pray then like this." I know this prayer has saturated my soul, heart, mind, and will because of its daily recitation. As long as I can remember, long before I could understand what it all meant, our family said the Lord's Prayer each night before going to bed. As a result every time I say it I see myself as a little boy bundled in floppy-footed pajamas cuddled up close to my parents, feeling my father's warm breath and my mother's tender hug, yawning halfway through. Even today I still hear their gentle voices in the background whispering, "Brush your teeth, brush your teeth." Thus dentistry and theology have always created an odd sort of blend in my spiritual life. When I graduated from high school and went off to college, the daily recitation of the Lord's Prayer went from English to Greek, since old Dr. Gammie had us say it as the opening prayer in class every day, a tradition I have continued whenever I teach Greek. Years ago, Dr. Gammie died of cancer, but his "Πάτερ ἡμῶν [Pater Hemon]" still lives on in me.

Pater Hemon. It's as near to me as my father and my mother. Maybe that's why Jesus started it off, "Pray then like this: Our Father who art in heaven." Notice that the first word in Greek is Father: *Pater.* What a startling thing it must have been for Jesus to begin the model prayer in this way, since it would have sounded irreverent and entirely too familiar. Dr. George Buttrick was such an imposing and powerful force in so many people's lives, such a great preacher and church leader, that no one ever imagined calling him anything but "Dr. Buttrick." When someone asked, "What's his first name?" the reply was "Dr." That only gives you a taste of what it was like to address the Creator of the universe. God was so holy and removed that you didn't even say God's name. Tell them that "I am who I am" has sent you. And yet, Jews longed to talk to God intimately at any time, even though God struck them strangely mute. According to James Charlesworth, "Jesus' Prayer, the Lord's Prayer, was a model for such personal and spontaneous prayers. Like other personal prayers, it is brief, couched in a simple style, and addresses God in the second person. It was the outline to be used when praying spontaneously."[3]

The Greeks and the Romans had their own views of God. Pagan incantations called on all the gods, hoping that one of the names would claim attention of the proper deity. In other words, they were covering their bases like people who join lots of different denominations throughout their lives in a kind of theological hedging of bets. The Jews had different words for God, like Elohim and Adonai, but the name of God was actually unpronounceable for fear they might be accused of blaspheming. Yet Jesus starts his prayer with this tender, warm salutation to the Supreme Being by simply saying, "Father." Greeks and Romans would never have done that. The Aramaic is Abba. In Arabic it's Yabba and the only possible English translation is "Daddy." "Daddy," Jesus says to God, which is OK for Jesus, the Son of God. "Father, if it be possible, let this cup pass from me." "Father, forgive them, for they know not what they do." Sure, that's fine for Jesus to call God "Father," but what about the rest of us? He has us all starting off our prayer to God with this very intimate word, which in essence means, "Hey, Dad, can we talk?"

Contrast this approach with the story of Prometheus, one of the Greek gods, who felt sorry for men and women because we didn't have fire, took fire from heaven, and gave it to humanity. But Zeus, the king of the gods, was so mad about this that he chained Prometheus to a rock in the middle of the Adriatic, where Prometheus was tortured by the heat and thirst of the day and by the cold of the night. In addition, Zeus sent a vulture to tear out Prometheus's liver, which grew again, only to be torn out again. The Greek, Roman, and Aztec gods were jealous, vengeful, and demanding. Even the Hebrew God had traits like these, although Yahweh could also be more loving and merciful.

Contrast this ancient view of God as a giant frown in the sky to the beginning of Jesus' model prayer: "Daddy, are you there? Hey, Dad, can we talk?" Of course, Jesus did not mean by this familiarity to remove the majesty and power of God. All Jesus did was to make the majesty and power of God more approachable. Barclay loved to recount the story of the Roman emperor marching in all his glory in a great victory parade. The streets were lined with cheering crowds. As they rode by where the empress and her young son were sitting in review, suddenly the boy sprang from his seat, wormed his way through the crowd, scampering between startled legionnaires to meet his father's chariot. One soldier finally caught him and said, "You can't do that, boy. Don't you know that's the emperor in that chariot?" The little boy laughed. "He may be your emperor, but he's my daddy!"[4] God may be the ruler over all nature and history, but God is still our

Father. To call God Father at the beginning of this prayer is to define our relationship to God. It is to say that we don't have to go through ten administrative assistants to get to the God of the universe—that God is as close to us as a parent. With God, there is no call-waiting and no voice mail. God is there waiting for us.

Oswald Hoffmann is right when he says that God "is not a moody and capricious Father—not like some human fathers, on one day and off the next. God has one prevailing mood: love, for God *is* love."[5] God's judgments and actions always demonstrate a loving purpose. You know what it's like when someone is "for" you and not "against" you. You can even take occasional criticism and gentle correction from someone who is "for" you.

However, this analogy still causes difficulties for some people. Some have problems with the maleness and the obvious patriarchy that "Father" implies in reference to God. One way to overcome that is to remember that language for God in the Bible is symbolic, not a literal description of the true nature of God. For others the problem with using the word "Father" while talking about or addressing God is that we unconsciously tuck into it the various imperfections of our own fathers. As wonderful as some of our fathers are and have been, not one of them has ever been perfect; and yet we tend to transfer all our human experiences with our own fathers to God every time we pray the Lord's Prayer. We can't help ourselves. For some it's a very serious matter, especially if they were ever sexually, physically, or emotionally abused by their fathers. A few years ago my wife, Jane, was helping a woman who had come to the Genesis Women's Shelter in Dallas, Texas, a home for battered women and children. One day Jane was babysitting the woman's four-year-old daughter, Christine, and brought her by our house to swing on our backyard swing. When I appeared and tried to say hello, the little girl clutched Jane's leg tightly and stared at the ground, counting her shoelaces. I've seen shy children before, but never anyone as reticent as this. No amount of clowning or funny faces on my part made any difference. Later Jane told me some of the awful things that had happened to her and how she had no idea of what a kind man could be like. Imagine Christine going to church and praying this prayer, "Our Father who art in heaven." What is she going to think about God? There are no doubt grown-up Christines sitting in every church, still staring at the floor. For some, God as Daddy isn't so good.

French worker-priest Pierre Raphael, cofounder of Abraham House in the South Bronx, served as a chaplain to prisoners on Rikers Island in New York. Raphael recounts how thousands of his imprisoned flock saw *father* as a curse word because of either abandonment or abuse. "How is it possible," writes Raphael, "under such conditions, to proclaim and offer the blessed words, 'heavenly father,' when even the most tenuous relationship to a father is missing . . . ? How is it possible to make the leap from these cages and these wounds to a God who wants to be close to us and make known the joy he has for us?"[6]

So, the whole idea of God and Daddy has to be changed. I think that's in part what Jesus is doing by starting this prayer with such an intimate and personal opening. "Daddy, are you there? Hey, Dad, can we talk?" The good dads are always there, always listening when we call in the middle of the night. Do you see how Jesus' use of "Daddy" in this prayer transcends all our typical understandings of fatherhood? It's certainly not merely maleness or just parenthood that he's trying to communicate here. It's love in action and the perfect freedom to come to God at any place and any time and the fact that God is as near to us as the breath we breathe. God is sitting next to you in the pew, riding along in the car with you. There is no busy signal with this God, no fourteen automated messages you have to listen to before you get through. God handles all incoming calls simultaneously, and the calls are always toll-free.

What do we have to do? We need to listen. That's why Jesus put God, not us, first in the prayer, because prayer is primarily listening to God, not the other way around. A woman calls her father. She hasn't talked to him for a while. "Daddy," "Susan." The words tumble out from both simultaneously tripping over each other. Both start talking at the same time. "You go first." "No, you first." "No, you." "No, it's all right." Finally she insists. "Daddy, I want to hear what you have to say. Please, Daddy, you go first." Prayer is saying to God, "Daddy, you go first. I want to hear what you have to say."

So Jesus started his prayer "Daddy," but qualified it by adding this phrase to help us see how "our" God is no ordinary parent: "Our Daddy who art in heaven." What do you suppose he meant by heaven? Not just the celestial city with golden streets. What is heaven for you? The perfect day that never ends, with someone you really love? The quality of life toward which we are all striving? I'll tell you what I think it is. I think it's a place where no one is ever alone again and all the barriers are broken down between us: husbands and wives, parents and children, races and nations. I believe that's why Jesus says, not just "Father," but "Our Father." By adding the "our," he immediately places us in the middle of the whole human family, whether we like it or not. Now it's no longer "my" prayer to "my" God, but "our" prayer to "our" father. For to pray "our" Father is to recognize that we are all children of God: red and yellow, black and white, we are all precious in God's sight. To pray to "our" Father is to recognize that under God we are brothers and sisters one to another, no matter how much we may disagree. When we pray "Our" Father we recognize that God belongs to all of us, or rather all of us belong to God. Where does this take us ethically and morally? To a place that lifts us out of our natural selfish tendencies, a place that reminds us that real friendship in Christ means we have the right to disagree, knowing that mutual respect and affection are not at stake. Why? Because God is "our" Father, that is, the Father of all of us.

Since heaven is the place where all differences are dropped and all peoples come together, "Our Father who art in heaven" is the one who brings us together, and every time God does we get glimpses of heaven here on earth. That's why later Jesus adds that phrase "on earth as it is in heaven."

I saw it a few years ago when Fred Craddock was the Brown Lecturer at First Presbyterian Church in Dallas. I decided to go all out and invite a wide spectrum of religious leaders from around the city to the ministers' luncheon. People said to me, "You'll never get that list of preachers together in the same room! One pastor from the moderate Park Cities Baptist Church; the dean of the Episcopal cathedral; S. M. Wright, that enormous black preacher whose raspy and booming voice when he spoke sounded like the very voice of God; a Roman Catholic priest; the radical feminist female pastor of the First Unitarian Church; and W.A. Criswell, the conservative pastor of First Baptist Church, all in the same room? It will never happen!" they said. But it did. I made sure Dr. Criswell was seated next to the radical feminist Unitarian pastor, then watched it all from the other end of the

table. It was a sight to see, all those ecclesiastical fireworks. "OUR
Father who art in heaven"—hardly.

"First time in forty-six years I've ever been in this church," said
Dr. Criswell, whose church was right down the street. "Could you
show me the sanctuary?" I did, and he loved it. He stood for a long
time staring at the dome in a kind of holy awe. Then he made his way
slowly up into the pulpit. "You know what I'd really like to see—the
Stewpot where you feed hundreds of poor, hungry people every day."
As we made our way into the bowels of the church (the location of the
Stewpot at that time), where the world's homeless ate every day, and
went through the dental clinic, he was moved to tears. No one had ever
seen him attend an ecumenical event like this, especially not to stay
once he saw who all was there. But he did and he wrote me these
words in a letter: "With all my heart, thank you for including me in
that profitable luncheon yesterday at noon. The whole session was one
of the most interesting I have ever attended." People asked me later,
"How did you get W.A. Criswell and all those preachers in that same
room together?" I replied, "It didn't have anything to do with me or
Fred Craddock. It was 'Our Father who art in heaven,' showing us
here and now what heaven will be like someday." No wonder Jesus
said, "Pray then like this: Our Father who art in heaven . . ."

Questions for Discussion

1. How often do you talk to God? When you do, is your inter-
   change conversational, formulaic, or spontaneous?
2. Does the idea of addressing God as Father make you feel closer
   to God or more distant and removed? Explain.
3. Does sharing God with others by praying "*Our* Father" feel like
   an intrusion on your personal time with God, or does it broaden
   your understanding of private prayer done in the context of community? Explain.
4. Does the Lord's Prayer change or enhance your view of heaven?
   If so, in what ways?

3

Hallowed Be Thy Name

ἁγιασθήτω τὸ ὄνομά σου

ΔΓΙΔϹΘΗΤѠ ΤΟ ΟΝΟΜΔ ϹΟΥ

*H*allowed is not a word we use very often in normal conversation. It's not a word we hear much on TV or the radio, either, or anywhere except in church. Perhaps that's the reason for the story about a boy asking his Sunday school teacher one morning why God's name was Harold. "What do you mean?" "Well," said the boy, "every time we pray the Lord's Prayer we say, 'Harold be thy name!'"

Hallowed is just not a word you hear very much. It's one of those old-fashioned words that means holy, ἁγιάζω (*hagiozo*) in Greek. Holy, special, different. We may not use the word, but we understand what it means. A hallowed or holy place is a special place that can bring back all kinds of memories every time you see or just think about it, like the house you grew up in. It wasn't much but it seemed like a mansion to you. Or the place you met a certain friend, one you've kept up with all your life or maybe the one you married. Our lives are home movies of all the people we've ever been, the people we've ever known, and all the places and moments in our lives that define who we are today. Most of these events seem like "only yesterday." "Hallowed be those memories." It's a holy time when you think back on them. If a fire suddenly engulfed your house and you had to get out right now, what would you grab, what would you take? Whatever it is, it's something that is very dear to you, hallowed, special, and dear to your heart.

Hallowed means "respected," the way we respect certain people whether they are living or dead, people whose names we cannot say without getting a lump in our throats, people in our families and our churches that we have known all our lives. They were with us for a time touching our lives in special ways and now suddenly they are gone, but their memories linger. Hallowed be their names. Not that they were saints so much as that they trigger in us certain feelings of joy, peace, and hope. They were different somehow, special.

Certain names have a way of doing that, especially names in the Bible. After all, in the biblical world a name was very important because it always told you something about the person. Isaac's name meant "laughter," because Abraham and Sarah had a good laugh about the fact that God was finally going to give them a child in their old age. Jonah meant "dove" in Hebrew and "dove" was a symbol for Israel, which had not shared the word of God with the world and thus was swallowed up by the great fish—Babylon and so forth. You get the point. The names of biblical characters described who they were and the very essence of their being. Even in our time names have the power to arouse deep feelings and different feelings because they represent different realities: Lincoln, Hitler, Mother Teresa. So also the name of God, which was for biblical folks so special and so holy they couldn't even utter it. So they hallowed the name. They treasured it and kept it quiet like some sort of secret password, for fear they might smudge it if they said it or used it incorrectly. Implicit in this petition, "Hallowed be thy name," was a significant characteristic in Jewish ethics. For example, rabbis subsequent to Jesus believed that people who did not pay their bills on time profaned and smudged the name of God.[1]

Names can be smudged by certain acts. "Don't you have any respect for the dead?" they said to old man Blakeslee in Olive Ann Burns's *Cold Sassy Tree*. When his wife, Matty Lou, was dying, old man Blakeslee decided to marry Miss Love Simpson even before Matty Lou was gone. And as soon as she died he asked Miss Love, while folks were still wearing black. Why, her body was still warm, and you just didn't do a thing like that in a small Georgia town! In fact, you just didn't do it at all except in places like Las Vegas and New York City. His daughters and friends were saying, "Don't you have any respect for the dead? Can't you hallow her name? Don't you see you're smudging her good name by marrying so quickly?

Hallowed be her name." But he didn't listen. He married Miss Love, and both his name and hers got smudged in the process. In a small town like that your name was very important.[2] It's even more important in big towns. If your name gets smudged, it's a stain that is not easily erased in the public psyche. Just ask Martha Stewart or Enron.

But how do we smudge the name of God? By not living up to what God calls us to do or say. Stop and think. In your relationship to family and friends or in your business, are you hallowing and honoring the name of God, or are you smudging it? All through the Bible, folks smudged the name of God by their actions. Cain, Jacob, Moses, David, Peter. You remember all their stories and how they kept letting God down no matter how hard they tried to be good.

Praying, "Hallowed be thy name" means not letting God down, not smudging the name of God. Will Willimon tells of the college student who was the first one in his family to go to college. When someone offered the student illegal drugs with the taunt, "Go ahead, try it. It'll make you feel good," and the student said "No," the drug dealer continued, "Don't be so uptight. Nobody's going to know you tried a little dope. . . ." "That's not the point," said the student. "The point is that my mother cleaned houses and washed floors to send me to college. I am here because of her. I am here for her. I wouldn't do anything that might demean her sacrifice for me."[3]

So with us. When we steal, cheat on our marriages or our income tax, or put others down we are smudging the good name of God, who sacrificed everything for us that we might have life. Praying "Hallowed be thy name" and living it means not smudging God's name with our words or our actions. Praying "Hallowed be thy name" reminds us that our first words to God should be in praise of God's holy name, in other words, the very essence of God that fills our lives. So often we treat God at the beginning of our prayers the way we used to treat our fathers or mothers when they came home from a long trip. Usually, the first thing out of our mouths was, "Daddy, Daddy [or Mommy, Mommy], what did you bring me?" when it should have been, "Daddy [or Mommy], I'm so glad to see you!" In other words, so often we run to God asking for this and that first, when we should be thanking God for who God is and enjoying being with God and experiencing God's blessings.

Of course, Jesus showed us how to honor God, to hallow God and God's name by the way he prayed and the way he lived his whole life. He knew that being away from God too often was like shutting yourself off completely from the warmth of the sun. Eventually your life turns cold and dark. Jesus understood what it meant to be in the presence of God on a regular basis and to humbly thank God for life itself. All the way to the cross, Jesus hallowed the name of God. So also we should hallow God's name.

But if you read the text closely enough you will see that it's not we who do the hallowing, but God who does it through us. The petition is put in the passive voice and comes out literally something like this: "May your name be hallowed," and you could add the phrase, "in the way we live our lives." The whole petition would then read, "May your name be hallowed, O God, in the way we live our lives."

God's name, then, is not something we possess, but an action by God that transforms our lives by giving us new names, new identities, and new destinies. Ebeling puts it this way: "The hallowing of the name is not something additional over and above God's name; it means, rather, that God's name becomes event and thereby God *happens.*"[4] And in this "happening" God steps out of the divine anonymity and brings us out of our anonymity as well, telling us who we really are and what we really are supposed to be doing with our lives. In other words, through the power of the Holy Spirit the hallowing of God's name turns us into new creations altogether.

Do you see now? The burden for the hallowing is put on God. We don't do the hallowing. God does it to us, around us, and through us. We don't begin with our holiness, but with God's becoming holy to us and in us. So how do we hallow God's name? By allowing God to work through our lives and by seeing life itself, not as just one darn thing after another and then you die, but as God's precious and holy gift to us every single day. In other words, we hallow God's name by seeing all of life as extraordinary. Praying this petition means treasuring every moment, every affiliation and circumstance in life, as a gift from God. Everything becomes holy because it belongs to God, which transforms our way of thinking. The eighteenth-century Jesuit Jean-Pierre de Caussade, called it the sacrament of the present moment,[5] for God blesses every second.

This is what it takes to be a part of God's kingdom, and no one should feel rushed into it. I remember years ago, in a church I was serving, a couple had been visiting for months and lots of people had been badgering them to join. "You haven't joined yet?" They were getting a little gun-shy. One day when one of the church members walked up to them and greeted them boldly in the parlor, they said, "We're not ready to join," to which the church member replied, "Oh, I know that. I'm not sure you qualify." Now that's an interesting approach to evangelism—a little reverse psychology! But it raises a good question. How do you qualify? A good answer might be by hallowing God's name in the way you live your life: by committing to a new way of life that sees God blessing and hallowing every moment, by surrendering your life not just to Christ, but to a new Christlikeness full of joy and hope.

Karl Barth points out that when we speak of God, the name or ὄνομα (*onoma*) of God points to the "glorious representation of God in the created world." And we, God's creatures, are bearers of God's name. Furthermore, the very fact that we are praying "Hallowed be thy name" means that God's name is already known to us—a name that is above every name.[6] Both Augustine and Cyprian remind us that it's not a question whether or not God's name in itself is hallowed— that is a fact. The question is whether God's name is made holy in us, and that thereby the world understands by seeing us the holiness of God's name.[7] That's where we come into the picture. When we truly believe in "Our Father who art in heaven," we make God's holy name visible with our actions and our words, like the saints in stained-glass windows through which the light of God shines. This process of hallowing God's name is a form of onomatopoeia if you take the literal meaning of the word from *onoma* (name) and *poieo* (make). What does this mean? As we hallow God's name, God sanctifies our lives by making a name for us, a new name if you will, whose sound and very existence points to peace and joy and hope.

The problem is we don't follow through, which turns this petition into a prayer of confession, because we are aware of our own sin. Luther believed that this phrase in the Lord's Prayer puts us in our places. It reminds us how often we fall short by not hallowing God's name. So we move from prayer of praise and thanksgiving in the opening line, "Our Father who art in heaven," to an act of penitence, "Hallowed be thy name," because we don't do it very well. We break the commandments by having other gods and taking the name of God in vain in the ways we mistreat our friends and neighbors and especially the poor.[8] On our own, we will never be able to live "hallowed" lives that put God first and glorify God's name in the world. Only God working in and through us to sanctify us through the atoning sacrifice of Jesus Christ and the indwelling power of the Holy Spirit can truly help us hallow God's name.

What Jesus is talking about in this petition is not just positive thinking; it's hallowed thinking and hallowed living. It's having your jubilee in easy reach. Now there's an odd phrase. One of our sons came up to me once when he was in elementary school and said, "Dad, is your jubilee in easy reach?" I replied, "Is this a trick question?" "No," he said, "it means, are you happy? Don't you remember how Ruth, the old black maid in Bette Greene's book *Summer of My German Soldier*, asked Patty this question?"[9] Sure enough, I did remember, since we had all read it as part of his homework. What a great question. Is your jubilee in easy reach? There are some people who always seem to have their jubilee in easy reach no matter what is going on their lives, good or bad. These are people who see all of life as extraordinary, who live life to the fullest even in the midst of deep pain. These are the ones who know that when we pray "Hallowed be thy name" we are asking God to fill us with divine presence and power. Discouragement over the past and worry over the future fade in the enjoyment of the present.

Truly praying "Hallowed be thy name" means that we accept each day as a precious gift from God. Every person we meet, even the nettlesome ones who teach us humility and patience, suddenly become a special present from God, each wrapped up in the unique clothing of a distinctive personality. It means that our work becomes a privilege and not just a tiresome burden. It means that old tasks are done with a new enthusiasm, and every problem becomes an opportunity and every obstacle a challenge. A kiss good-bye in the morning, a little call to a friend during the day, an "I'm thinking of you" note, all may seem ordinary to us, but for the one on the receiving end it brings that person's jubilee within easy reach. In short, a life hallowed by God's name is an extraordinary life composed of what to others might seem like millions of very ordinary moments. To pray "Hallowed be thy name" is to see God hallowing the ordinary everyday moments of our lives.

A man named Bob knew how to hallow every day of his life as well as anyone I have ever known. He was dying of a brain tumor, but full of more life than most people I know who are completely healthy. "How are you, Bill?" he would ask with a smile that lit up his face. "Don't worry about me. I've got these tapes I'm listening to. I've got my friends and my faith. What more could you ask for?" he always said with that huge grin. Just to be with Bob always brought your jubilee "within easy reach" because he was one who saw every moment, every word as a precious gift from God. The last time I saw him alive he said to me, "Hey, Bill, you know what I dreamt the other night?" I said, "No, Bob, what?" He said, "I dreamt that I saw God, and you'll never guess what God did. He gave me a high five!" Now there was a man who knew what it meant to pray and to live "Our Father who art in heaven, *hallowed be thy name*" (italics ours).

Questions for Discussion

1. Name some of the persons in your life, whether still living or not, who have touched you in special ways, and talk about why they are so important.
2. Remember holy and unique moments that were turning points in your life, and try to remember why. What was so extraordinary about them?
3. How is God working in and through you now to sanctify your life so that when you pray, "Hallowed be thy name," you see the impact your life is making on others?
4. Is your "jubilee within easy reach," and if not, why not?

4

Thy Kingdom Come

ἐλθέτω ἡ βασιλεία σου

ＥΛΘΕＴＷ Η ＢᴧＣΙᴧＥΙᴧ ＣΟＹ

I don't know if the mountain sermon from which this prayer came was given at one shot or not. Scholars argue about it, so we'll leave them to their arguing. It's probably a compilation of the best of Jesus from several sermons on several different occasions. Whatever the case, I want you to imagine yourself in first-century Palestine, having been dragged by a neighbor to hear some carpenter talk about something besides the latest wood-working techniques. This morning he's going on about prayer, a real cure for insomnia. He's teaching everyone a new prayer that starts "Our Father who art in heaven, hallowed be thy name," then he adds the next phrase, "Thy kingdom come. . . ."

Suddenly your neighbor punches you in the ribs because you have dozed off, the way people in church always do, and whispers, "Hey, did you hear that? Sound familiar?"

"Hear what?" you reply, rubbing the sleep from your eyes. After all, the night before was a long one; you'd really tied one on, and frankly had planned on sleeping in this morning until your friend had pushed you out of bed, pumped you with coffee, and hauled you out to this hillside to hear this guy who frankly hasn't wowed you yet. He isn't like the other speakers you've heard through the years, hellfire-and-brimstone preachers like John the Baptist, who could command a crowd's attention at a moment's notice. But there was something different about this one. Not an arrogant bone in his body. There is nothing flashy about him. No booming, commanding voice. No piercing eyes. And yet, there is a simple radiance, like the kind

/ 23

you've seen on a woman's face when she was holding a baby she'd just delivered, or the peaceful look on a man's face right before he died. That's what it was—the look on this young man's face when he uttered these simple words, "Thy kingdom come."

"Doesn't that ring a bell?" says your friend. "Here, finish your latte and wake up. It'll come to you." But it isn't coming, not just yet. "Thy kingdom come." . . . Hmmm. Yes, it does sound familiar, but from where? The sunlight breaks through the clouds and causes temporary blindness as you squint at the silhouette of the man on the hill. "Think, dummy," says your friend. "When was the last time you were in the synagogue? It's the first and second petition of the Kaddish, pronounced by the rabbi at the conclusion of the synagogue service and often at the end of the prayers: 'May God establish his kingdom in your lifetime and in your days and in all the ages of the whole house of Israel soon and in the near future.'"

That's when it hits you. It all comes back to you suddenly. "Hey, you're right," you say to your friend. "It is the same. This Jesus guy has just borrowed his stuff from the synagogue prayers and is out here passing it off as something new." But as you listen you realize that it really is new, that there is something different about this young rabbi and his little prayer, something remarkably different. Sure, he talks about hallowing God's name, but before that he said God's name and actually called God "Daddy," "Papa." No respectable rabbi would ever do that! And when he talked about the kingdom it was clear he meant more than Israel. He certainly wasn't referring to Rome. So what kind of kingdom is he talking about? Suddenly you realize there's something radically different going on here.

One St. Patrick's Day a fellow had on orange instead of green, since Protestants wear orange on St. Patrick's, and someone said, "That's not quite green," and the fellow replied, "Yeah, well I'm not quite Catholic." Jesus was Jewish, but not quite. There was something different about him and certainly something different about the kingdom to which he was referring.

"Thy kingdom come." What does it mean? Not what you think on the surface, so we'll have to go a little deeper to figure out where he's going with this. Three points emerge as we look at this text, and this is the simplest outline you'll ever hear. The first point is simply "Thy."

THY kingdom come. From the very beginning, Jesus is putting us in our place, stripping us of any notion that we're going to have any say at all in what this new kingdom is going to look like or how it's going to be put together.

Jesus knows if we had our way we'd rather pray, "Our Father who art in heaven, hallowed be thy name, MY kingdom come, MY will be done, on earth as it is in heaven." But no, says Jesus, it's not your kingdom or mine, it's God's. "THY kingdom come." What a startling change! We have gone from the warm and comfortable baby talk of "Our Father in heaven, with a name that is hallowed" to guess what—you are not in charge? That's one of the first things older brothers and sisters learn when a new baby is born. The new baby comes along and knocks them off their throne, which leads to sibling rivalry that started with Cain and Abel and continued from Jacob and Esau to Joseph and all his envious brothers. It's familial conflict born of envy that keeps getting recycled from one generation to the next. Even the father gets dethroned when a new baby enters the household. And sooner or later the new baby learns it too from a neighbor or a teacher or a coach: eventually we all get knocked off our thrones. This whole process represents a re-forming and a trans-forming of one's ego, the socialization of the essence of your personality to a new way of thinking and living.

It's the move from thinking you're somebody to feeling like a nobody, as someone puts you in your place. When Adlai Stevenson was running for President, he had just finished a speech when a woman gushed up to him and said, "Mr. Stevenson, that speech was absolutely superfluous!" to which he replied, "Thank you, I'm thinking of having it published posthumously," and she said, "Great, the sooner, the better!" The Christian life is a very long, sometimes painful but ultimately joyful, process of being dethroned. We go through it all the time. Parents are dethroned by children who outdo them, and retirees are dethroned by retirement itself when they go around the office and nobody cares what they think anymore. We spend our whole lives getting dethroned, and it happens again with the coming of God's kingdom. To pray "*Thy* kingdom come" is to realize that you are no longer number one. You never have been. God is. And because God is, you should seek God's kingdom and not your own glory in the way you live your life, in the things you buy, the way you think about your career, and especially in the ways you treat those around you. Ask yourself this question: "In all I do and say am I seeking first the kingdom of God and God's righteousness, or my own glory?"

"Thy kingdom come" is about seeing everything as God's, not yours. We want to sing, "I did it my way," but this prayer wants us to sing, "I did it God's way." And with this little phrase, "thy kingdom come," Jesus is knocking the selfishness right out of our prayers and our lives and filling our minds not with what we want, but with what God wants for us and our world. He is *reorienting* our lives away from ourselves and our petty little worries about this or that, most of which is pretty trivial, and toward God. Jesus is saying, "Get your theology straight. See the world and your life in a totally different way when you pray and really believe 'THY kingdom come.'"

So, the first point is *"thy"* instead of "my." The second is *"kingdom,"* a word that usually causes us to recoil. The pharaohs in Egypt had a kingdom, but so did Solomon, so kingdoms in themselves are not inherently good or bad—it depends on who is in power. But kingdoms sound authoritarian to our Western ears. We believe in democracy and representative government. After all, our Constitution and three branches of government came right out of Calvin's and Knox's Presbyterian polity, with no king or queen or pope or bishop, and with checks and balances because we're all a little sinful and selfish—in other words, basically out for ourselves. So the word "kingdom" sounds to our ears not only a little too male chauvinist, but very undemocratic, to which Jesus replies, "Yeah, well, so what?" This is God's kingdom we're talking about, not yours. We've already established that fact. THY kingdom come, not mine or yours. Besides, Buechner reminds us, God's kingdom is not a place, it's a condition, a way of life.[1] God's kingdom is present wherever God's will is being done on earth, which is probably why this petition naturally morphs into the next one, "Thy will be done." "Thy kingdom come, thy will be done."

Where do we get glimpses of God's will being done, of God's kingdom coming on earth as it is in heaven? We see it all around us if our eyes are open and we are alert to it. We see it in the soup kitchens and the various clinics across the street where the hungry are fed, the naked clothed, and the sick healed. Father Pierre Raphael saw it every day at Rikers Prison. One year, on Ash Wednesday, a prisoner told him he was going to court that day. "Please give the ashes to my brother. He is incarcerated here. And he will give them to me when I come back from court." Raphael writes of the incident, "Such words, in a place where everything seems lost, are the result of countless graces." God's kingdom is truly coming.[2]

We see examples of God's kingdom all around us, but the idea Jesus is presenting is even deeper than that. It is God who is sovereign over all nature and history, exercising that sovereignty by moving among nations even as we speak, the Spirit of God brooding over the chaotic waters of creation and stilling the storms gradually, slowly, sometimes even painfully, bringing creation closer and closer to the hope of real peace on earth. Think back across the last couple of decades and try to remember how different our world was during the Cold War, how different it was in Eastern Europe and Russia prior to the fall of the Berlin Wall, how different it was in South Africa before the fall of apartheid. How could human beings have pulled off all that occurred there all by themselves? "Thy kingdom come." It's coming and it isn't. It's here and it isn't here all at the same time, which is the reason that we need to keep praying for God's kingdom to come. This petition in the Lord's Prayer gives us a taste of realized eschatology. The kingdom is here but not everybody sees it. Jesus said, "The kingdom of heaven is at hand." Yes, it is, but where? Do you see it in the world, in your community, in your life?

Sober historians and wise theologians like Reinhold Niebuhr remind us to be very careful about so readily assigning too much to any period of history, especially while you are still living in it. A century ago humanity thought the kingdom was coming and they were bringing it in. In fact, nineteenth-century liberalism built the structure of its theology on the idea of progress, thinking that via evolution society was just getting better and better, and the world was approaching a kind of earthly nirvana, that God's kingdom was coming in our midst. Think about the attitude in 1914 where there was a certain well-being, a relative comfort among the nations. They were living in the rarified air of euphoria, cherishing the delusion that the kingdom of God will be an earthly utopia where ease and comfort will reign throughout the world. Little did they know that World War I was right around the corner, just waiting to bloody the face of Europe. When they dubbed that global scrimmage "the war to end wars," little did they know that there was another one on the way. Then came the Depression and the Holocaust and the threat of nuclear annihilation. Little do we know what lies ahead for our world as we continue to enter this new millennium, even in a time when a modern-day version of ancient Babylon struggles to establish a constitution and a new age of freedom. "Thy kingdom come" means we approach each new day with an element of humility, knowing that God often surprises us with liberations that always go beyond our little human schemes or plans. "Thy kingdom come" means God is bringing justice, peace, reconciliation, and hope in ways that often transcend our abilities to comprehend it.

Praying "Thy kingdom come" means asking God to show us where and how it's coming. The reason we need God's help is that we can't find it on our own—it all depends on the lens you have on when you go looking for it. Too often we look for it among the shadows of passing traffic and the latest news on CNN. But those fancies are not the true Reality. We won't find it in reckless acquisition or in fame or fortune. As long as we look for it among our worldly delights, we will never find it. Jesus is not calling for some sort of gnostic retreat from the world, but asking us to put on new "kingdom" lenses that will allow us to see what is right there in front of us, God moving and transforming all creation.

Karl Barth, in one of his lectures, asks us to imagine him standing before a table saying, "We pray for the removal of this covering, which now conceals all things, as the cloth which covers this table. The table is underneath [he raps on the table]. You hear it. But you do not see it. You have only to remove the cloth to see it. We pray in order that the covering which still veils the reality of the Kingdom be removed. . . . All of God's depth is there. . . . Our personal life and that of our family, the life of the Churches, the political events, all these are the covering. The reality is beneath it. . . . We cannot be sure of our position when we read the newspapers, religious or otherwise. For us to see the reality, thy Kingdom must come, Jesus Christ must become visible, even as he was visible at Easter, even as he revealed himself to his apostles."[3]

Which brings us to the final point: "*come.*" "Thy kingdom COME." This gets very active and very personal. It moves us beyond the intellectual and the emotional. It moves us beyond the revelatory into the practical. It reminds us that church stuff isn't just for church. It's for all of life. To pray "thy kingdom come" means that *we have to participate* in *the coming of God's kingdom.* God brings this kingdom into the world through us as we seek first the kingdom of God and God's righteousness. What's the point here? It's very simple. Just because we see God moving in our world doesn't mean that we can get complacent or lazy and let God take care of it all. Why? Because there are two little words implied in this petition—they are "through me." "Thy kingdom come *through me.*"

In Luke 17:20–21 when the Pharisees asked Jesus, "When will the kingdom come?" he said, "You cannot tell by observation when the kingdom of God comes. There will be no saying, 'Look, here it is!' or 'There it is!' for in fact *the kingdom of God is within you.*" That's why we can't just point around the world to evidence of the kingdom out there. It's not just happening *out there.* It's happening right here, in us. The kingdom is not something that primarily has to do with countries and nations. It has to do with each of us and how we are living our lives. It's personal before it's global, because the kingdom demands your will, your heart, your life and mine. Only when each of us makes a personal decision and submission does the kingdom begin to come. So the Chinese Christians once prayed, "Lord, revive your church, beginning with me."

It's one thing to pray "thy kingdom come" through heads of government and business; it's quite another to pray, "Thy kingdom come through me." The only way it's really going to happen is for our little personal kingdoms of envy and jealousy and petty rivalries and greed to topple. But that's Christianity in a nutshell, isn't it? To pray "thy kingdom come" is to realize that you are no longer number one, God is. When you realize it, it's very liberating because it takes you off the judgment seat and the "I have to impress everyone seat" and turns your life, your future, and the future of this planet over to God.

Tom Long tells of a Sunday a friend of his was at church, and after the service noticed that another friend, whom he had not seen in a while, was sitting on the other end of his pew. As people were leaving the sanctuary, he slid down the pew and engaged his friend in conversation. They stayed there for a few minutes talking, until the sanctuary was almost emptied of people except for a couple of children who were, as children like to do, running around in the sanctuary. One of the children, a little boy, went up into the pulpit and peered out. He saw his mother, who had come to look for him, in the back of the church, and he shouted into the microphone, "Mommy, Mommy, look at me! Look at me!" Tom's friend looked at his companion, who then said, "I think I've heard that sermon before." God is looking around for us and all we can say is, "Mommy, Mommy, look at me!" But to pray, "Thy kingdom come" and truly mean it, is to take the focus off ourselves and say, "Mommy, Daddy, O hallowed one in heaven, now I'm looking at you."

When as a young man Peter Marshall left his beloved Scotland for good, not knowing if he would ever return, his mother gave him this little piece of advice: "Dinna forget your verse my laddie: 'Seek ye first the kingdom of God and his righteousness and all these things shall be added unto you.' Long ago I pit ye in the Lord's hands and no be takin' ye awa noo. He will tak' care o' you. Dinna worry."[4] To pray "Thy kingdom come," and mean it, is to know that in life and in death we belong to God, the one who loves us as we are and makes us better than we ever could be on our own.

Questions for Discussion

1. Can you remember times when you were dethroned in your life? What were they like? What did these sometimes painful experiences teach you about yourself and God?
2. Think about times when you witnessed God's kingdom coming on earth in your life and in the world. How were you able to recognize them? Did you share your recognition with others? Will you share your "sightings" of the kingdom in your midst with those around you next time you see them? If not, why not?
3. What are some ways that God's kingdom can come "through you"?

5

Thy Will Be Done

γενηθήτω τὸ θέλημά σου

ΓΕΝΗΘΗΤѠ ΤΟ ΘΕΛΗΜᴧ ϹΟΥ

*I*t naturally follows, doesn't it, that if God's kingdom is in the process of coming, then it must be God's will that's driving it. That would make sense. And since the kingdom is God's and not ours, so is "the will of God." Of course, we wish it weren't, because we'd rather pray, "My will be done." But that's not what Jesus said, even though his disciples would have preferred it, especially James and John jockeying for a place at Jesus' right hand. This petition, "Thy will be done," may be one of the hardest to accept in the entire prayer. The reason it's hard to accept is that it's nearly impossible to figure out exactly what God's will is.

Following 9/11 and Hurricane Katrina, televangelists had a field day pronouncing these events as God's judgment on sinners. Nothing could be farther from the truth. This is not the modus operandi of the God revealed in Jesus Christ. Certainly, we know that God wants us to live moral and upright lives. God wants us to take care of "the least of these." God wants us to help bring justice to the earth. We also know from a careful reading of history that nations that hadn't done these things eventually ended up weaker, like a tree that rots from within. Thus they were more vulnerable to attack from without. But did God cause those attacks? No. Did God's servants and spokespersons, in the form of the prophets, try to warn the people about the possibility of demise from without? Yes. Did the people listen? Usually not. Tragedies happen. Does God cause them? Hardly. Is God there to help us pick up the pieces when they do?

The whole of Scripture answers with a resounding "YES." God is the one who repeatedly turns "what others meant for evil" into something profoundly good. For proof, review the stories of Joseph, Job, and Jesus—from prison to prominence, from losing everything to having even more, from cross to resurrection. God doesn't just make lemonade out of lemons, God takes everything bad and makes it the best.

Such is the true will of God. In other words, God is always and forever "for" us. Wrap your mind around that idea. Surely you've experienced it at least once in your life. If not, open your eyes and pay attention. This is the way God's will works. Something goes wrong, and it will; if you live long enough, it will. Your spouse or friend dies and leaves you alone and you think life is over, only to find out that God is there to pick you up from the floor, dust you off, and get you going again. Does that mean that everything in your life is going to be perfect from then on? Of course not. But God will never, ever let you go. What's my point? It's that the only way to think about the will of God is positively. If that's the case, then why would we ever want to pray anything but, "Thy will be done"? Whatever it is, we are ready for it.

I agree with Will Willimon[1] when he suggests that one of the best stories in the Bible is the story of Joseph, who drove his big brothers up the wall with his Technicolor dream coat and his teacher's pet status. Those of us who are parents understand. We don't intend to favor one child over another, but sometimes it's hard not to. I mean, Joseph was nearly perfect and so much fun that Jacob gave him extra attention, and it made Joseph's brothers mad. Jacob loved them all, but there was an extra twinkle in the old man's eye whenever Joseph walked into the room.

As if that wasn't enough, Joseph started having those infernal dreams. No matter how many dreams you have about your glorious future, you ought to keep them to yourself unless you're on a psychiatrist's couch. But Joseph just couldn't stop talking. So picture it now. Here comes your kid brother walking toward you with that golden-boy swagger, as if the whole world revolved around him. Then he has the gall to say, "Listen to this, guys. I had a dream last night. We were binding sheaves of wheat in the field, and your sheaves bowed down to mine." "Oh, really?" said Joseph's brothers. "Then I dreamed that the sun, the moon, and the stars bowed down to me too." "Oh, you did, did you?" said his brothers. Then Joseph really sent them over the top when he said, "I wonder what Freud would say about my dream?" "We'll give him a dream, in fact a sure enough nightmare!" grumbled his brothers to themselves. So they sold him into slavery in Egypt. They put sheep's blood all over Joseph's fancy coat and gave it to their father, saying, "Guess what happened to Joseph today? Something came along and ate him!"

You know the rest of the story, how Joseph spent some time in an Egyptian slammer, but my guess is he had some of the same wheeler-dealer genes his old man had, and pretty soon he had all the guards laughing like Bill Murray's character at the mental hospital in the movie *What about Bob?* and before you could say "Jack Sprat" he'd been promoted to court psychiatrist and found himself interpreting Pharaoh's dreams. He was so good at it that Pharaoh even took Joseph at his word about the lean years to come and set up a huge endowment to cover the hard times ahead. Sure enough he was right, and before long his brothers, who thought he was long dead, found themselves on his doorstep, hat in hand, begging for grain. He'd changed so much and was such a big deal in Egypt that they didn't even recognize him. Instead of having their heads lopped off, he forgave them for what they'd done to him.

The biblical writer says Joseph summarizes it all astonishingly: "What others meant for evil, God meant for good." It's an amazing story about the loving grace of God to turn almost any sorry situation in which we find ourselves into something more beautiful than we could have ever imagined and certainly ever dreamed of. Time and time again God does it. Look at Noah, look at the once childless parents Abraham and Sarah. Look at the Israelites stuck in slavery. To pray, "Thy will be done," means above all else to believe at the very core of your being that God is going to surprise you in ways you never imagined. I don't know about you, but I think that's good.

Yet figuring out how God is going to do it, how it's going to happen, and what direction the twists and turns of our lives are going to take—that's another matter altogether. We have two problems with the will of God. One is discerning it and the other is doing it. Joseph seemed to be pretty good at doing both, at least in retrospect. But my guess is he was wondering what in the world had happened to him as he was jerked along in the chain gang on his way to Egypt. He must have been thinking: O brother, where art thou? and: O God, what is this all about?

The first problem is discerning the will of God. Mind you, it's not discerning that there *is* a will of God. That's hard to deny if you believe in God at all. There is no way we can escape the will of God. A fish might as well try to escape the sea in which it swims. You and I swim within the will of God every moment of every day. So, escaping the will of God is something we cannot do, but discerning it is something else altogether. The will of God is the hardest thing in the world to figure out.

People ask about it especially in the context of catastrophic suffering. They ask it about earthquake, tsunami, and hurricane victims. They ask it when their loved ones die. A young mother asked it of me nearly twenty years ago when her young husband went to an attic to get something and touched a live wire, He was gone in a flash, leaving her and her unborn child behind. She was several months along in her pregnancy and unable to climb the ladder, but kept calling her husband's name, "Ben, Ben, are you all right?" until she finally called a neighbor, who came over and found his lifeless body. "How does this fit into the will of God, Bill?" she asked with a blank look on her face.

What could I say? "Oh, sure, God meant to kill Ben because God had some special project for him in heaven"? Or, "God took him because he was a bad person and needed to be punished"? Anyone who knew her husband would have disagreed. No one's perfect. But Ben was as close as anyone I've ever known. So you play the part. You're the pastor or the friend holding the hand of the one left behind. What are you going to say to her about the will of God?

"Thy will be done," Jesus tells us to pray. "Thy kingdom come, thy will be done." How are we ever going to figure it out? How does the will of God relate to what we do or don't do in our lives? I do believe God calls us up short when we break certain laws. Break the law of gravity by jumping from the top of a six-story parking garage and you won't live to tell about it unless you've suddenly learned to fly. Cholesterol's too high? Blood pressure's over the top? Your pastor will probably be visiting you in the hospital after your stroke or heart attack. That's if you make it. If you don't, they will be saying some words over you as they put you into the ground.

I was leaving a hospital one day after calling on someone and barely got out the door before a man came up and said, "Hey, buddy, got a cigarette?"

I stopped and said, "Do I look as if I smoke? First of all, I don't smoke, and second, you shouldn't either."

"OK, sorry," he muttered, turning away.

"Don't you know Johnny Carson died young from smoking?"

"Young? I thought he was seventy-nine."

"Yeah, well, at fifty-six that sounds young to me!"

I thought about inviting him to church, but figured it might be a hard sell after that. I guess I was more into promoting proper behavior than evangelism that day. I felt like Moses hawking the Ten Commandments as I watched him walk away disheartened. People skills aside, the point is still on the mark. What's the point? Break God's laws, and sooner or later it will get you.

But here's the question that dogs most believers: Does God really pick out certain people to zap and others to leave alone? Because if God does that, then why do the good die young and the scoundrels survive? There's no way to figure it out. Jesus may want us to pray, "Thy will be done," but figuring out God's will is not all that easy. Both John Claypool and Rabbi Kushner[2] remind us that there is no way to answer the "Why Question." It's just not possible. "Why did Ben die like this?" his wife asked me pleadingly. I had to say, "I don't know, I just don't know," and felt very inadequate for it. After all, I'd been to seminary, have a PhD, have even taught in three seminaries and lectured at several more. I ought to have had all the answers, right? Wrong. I didn't have any answers, not a single one. Both as a pastor and as a theologian I felt completely helpless. Both Claypool and Kushner are right. There are no answers to the "Why" questions. We're just too small to take it all in. You might as well try to explain Einstein's theory of relativity to a small-neck crab. The immensity of the one transcends the capacity of the other.

So we find ourselves scoffing at Jesus' suggestion that we pray, "Thy will be done." Easy for you to say, Jesus. After all, you're the Son of God. You have a direct line to heaven. You get to sit at the right hand of the Creator. You already know the will of God. It's easy for you to pray, "Thy will be done." It's easy for you to say in the Garden, "Father, if it be thy will let this cup pass from me, but not my will but thine be done." Well, maybe that wasn't so easy to say after all. Yet you still had the inside track.

Being mere mortals, we can't figure out the will of God no matter how hard we try. So we moderns try to replace "thy will" with "my will be done," and create our own metaphors for life such as: Life is a party—grab all the gusto you can get! Life is a test—you either pass or fail. Life is a game where we try to win all the money, fame, and power we can. Life is a drama where we all play our parts while masking our deepest pains and fears. Life is absurd, a kind of Nietzschean nothingness where you live a few decades then you die—a journey from womb to tomb with only closed doors and dead-end streets. There's no will of God some people say, only your will and mine and the will of the people, whatever that means.

What is this elusive will of God, anyway? Well, for one thing it's not fate, not *Que sera sera*, "What will be will be," and all that. God is either active in nature and history, and sovereign over both, or not. "Thy will be done" means allowing our lives to become an arena for the activity of God, which gets played out in several different ways: there's the Intentional will of God, the Circumstantial or Permissive will of God, and the Ultimate will of God.

The Intentional will has to do with what God intends for our lives and our world. We've read Paul and know that "in everything God works for good with those who love [God], who are called according to [God's] purpose" (Rom. 8:28). We know that it's God's intention for the children of God to experience peace, joy, and hope. The Intentional will of God would never purposefully bring pain and suffering on any part of creation. God loves us too much for that. Besides, inflicting pain and suffering is just not part of the divine DNA.

The Circumstantial, Provisional, or Permissive, will of God means that we are not puppets—we have free will to choose and make mistakes. God's will allows for those mistakes and for catastrophic events. It's not that God causes plane crashes, earthquakes, tsunamis, or hurricanes, but God does allow them to happen. If God rescued us from every little or even big tragedy that occurred in our lives, it would deny our free will and turn us into little more than marionettes. Does that mean that God can't or won't even surprise us with miraculous turnarounds? Of course not. God is sovereign and can and will do whatever God wills. But we cannot predict when or how it happens. Thus, we live in the trust of the Ultimate will of God that eventually all things work together for good. "Thy will be done" means that we trust God to provide and to guide and to show us the way. God knows where we are going even before we do. God knows our tendencies and the kinds of trouble we're going to get into.

Such is the fable of the frog and the scorpion. We all know the story. The scorpion asks the frog for a ride across the river.

The frog scoffs, "I can't do that; you'll sting me on the back and I'll drown."

"Don't be a fool. If I stung you while riding on your back, I would drown too!"

The frog thinks for a moment and agrees. "Hop on."

The scorpion does so, and as the frog is swimming across, the scorpion stings him.

On his way down, the frog says, "Why did you sting me? You're going to die too."

Just before going under, the scorpion replies, "It's my nature to do so."

God knows our nature and sees the whole picture of our lives from beginning to end. It's not that God causes us to do good or bad, but God sees our propensities. I saw a billboard once that said, "First we form habits and then our habits form us." God sees where we are going. God is not surprised with the things we spend our money on or the ways we live our lives. The whole thing is laid out there before God like a jigsaw puzzle. A child works the puzzle, but at first the child doesn't know what it's supposed to be. The parent picks up the box cover that has fallen on the floor upside down and smiles. She knows how it's going to end up. Now the child, like all human beings, has the free will to put the pieces in this way and that, never the same way twice, sometimes taking longer to get to the right connections, sometimes getting frustrated. But all along God is watching, smiling, knowing how the whole thing is going to turn out eventually.

However, I don't think God is merely an absentee landlord or a grinning parent peeking over our shoulder. I believe that periodically God reaches over and says, "Why don't you try that piece there."

When we do, everything suddenly begins to come together. It may be a helping hand during the day, a kind word from a friend, a corrective nudge that we really needed to hear. Periodically, God's will is like the veritable brick wall we all run into sooner or later, that irresistible force, that "push back" that says, "I think you're going the wrong direction in your life and you really ought to stop and reevaluate it. Yes, I mean right now." For the prodigal son, it was the day he "came to himself." For Jonah, it was the day he realized he'd been swallowed up not by some huge fish, but by life itself. It was Melville's mythic *Moby Dick* or Hemingway's *Old Man and the Sea*. Praying "Thy will be done" and meaning it is a scary thing, because sooner or later it means that the God of the universe will be in your face, trying to break your will and bend it to God's as if you were some wild stallion on the loose. I know I've mixed metaphors from the sea to the plains, but you get the point. To pray "Thy will be done" and mean it is to recognize that God is present in your life, pushing you back almost like the neighborhood bully, trying to get your attention. Perhaps we see only in retrospect where and how God was active in our lives, through those *kairos* moments that are full of meaning and hope, as God opens for us new vistas through serendipitous brushes with the divine as our lives are played out in the mind and will of God.

To pray "Thy will be done" and mean it as we put our whole trust in God is to know that God is letting us go and letting us have our way by giving us room to maneuver within the divine field of consciousness. It means knowing that, as the apostle Paul found, "out of our weakness" God's "power is made perfect." It means that once we begin to discern the will of God for our lives we have to begin doing it, because we can't help ourselves. Living in the will of God, then, means faithfulness and perseverance in our pilgrimage; it means journeying to a destination rather than being pushed in whatever directions the winds of society or peer pressure blow. It means not just a desperate hanging on, but moving from strength to strength as in Romans 5:3–5 where we "rejoice in our sufferings, knowing that suffering produces endurance, and endurance produces character, and character produces hope, and hope does not disappoint us." Living in the will of God means prolonged obedience in the same direction.

God's will provides for us an organizing center around which we can build long and happy lives.

As with "Thy kingdom come," so God's will is done through you and me. We are the ones who fulfill God's will in the world. William Willimon tells of the peace demonstration where the police moved in to break the will of the crowd and disperse them, but just as the confrontation ensued a protestor shouted, "Quick, everyone to your knees, let's pray!" Above the commotion, someone started in, "Our Father . . . , thy will be done . . . ," which brought the police advance to a halt as some of officers joined the crowd in the prayer. What had begun as a heated altercation had now suddenly turned into something else altogether.[3] Such is the power of this little prayer. "Thy kingdom come, thy will be done" through you and through me.

Questions for Discussion

1. Look back on your life and think of the times when you sensed the will of God at work in you.
2. How do you think the will of God is present in tragic events in the world? Why do you think some good people die young and some who aren't so good seem to live long lives?
3. How does praying "Thy will be done" change your view of God's activity in your life and all creation?
4. How is God using you to fulfill God's will on earth?

6

On Earth as It Is in Heaven

ὡς ἐν οὐρανῷ καὶ ἐπὶ γῆς

ⲰⲤ ⲈⲚ ⲞⲨⲢⲀⲚⲰ ⲔⲀⲒ ⲈⲠⲒ ⲄⲎⲤ

While looking at this petition, I noticed something I'd never thought about before. The Greek for this phrase says literally, "as in heaven so also on earth." But most of the translations turn this phrase around and make it "on earth as it is in heaven." Most of them start with earth then move to heaven. But the Greek has the reverse, ὡς ἐν οὐρανῷ καὶ ἐπὶ γῆς (*hos en ourano kai epi ges*). As in heaven so also on earth. Just out of curiosity I checked Spanish, German, French, and Russian translations to see how they translated it. Spanish keeps the order we find in the Greek text: "*como en el cielo, así tambien en la tierra.*" Likewise, the German version is "*wie im Himmel, so auch auf Erden,*" "as in heaven so also on earth." But the French goes with more recent English translations, "*sur la terre comme au ciel.*" And the modern Russian version is, like the French, "*na zemle kak na nebe,*" "on earth as it is in heaven."

What's going on here? Why do some translations start with heaven and others start with earth? The truth is I don't know the answer. Maybe it flows better in English and French and Russian to say "on earth as it is in heaven." Or maybe it has something to do with the way different cultures think about the universe. Maybe people who are of English, French, or Russian backgrounds start their thinking about existence with what's going in their earthly existence, whereas Hispanic and German cultures would rather begin thinking about their lives and the history and the future of the world by first putting their focus on heaven.

/ 40

Whatever the case, we're starting with heaven because that's the way the Greek text starts, ὡς ἐν οὐρανῷ καὶ ἐπὶ γῆς. The first question we have to ask is, "What is heaven, anyway?" If we're praying fervently for God's kingdom to come and God's will to be done "as in heaven so also on earth," it might be ·a good idea to know what heaven is, since we're praying for God to bring its joys to earth. What is heaven for you, and are you really ready for it?

A preacher asked his congregation one morning, "Will all those who are going to heaven please stand up?" Everyone in the congregation stood up except for one man, who remained seated quietly in the second pew.

The preacher looked at the man quizzically. "Aren't you going to heaven?"

"Sure I am, preacher, but I figured you were getting a group up to go right now!"

We all want to go to heaven someday, but what about having heaven come here? Are we sure we're ready for that? If we are praying that God's kingdom come and God's will be done as it is in heaven so also on earth, we'd better know what this heaven is in the first place.

What is heaven for you? Is it the fount of enlightenment or the fulfillment of all your hopes and desires? Or is heaven for you perpetual mirth, with a fiddle that never stops playing for dancers who never tire? "I can tell you what it would be for me," said someone whose body was racked with pain every day "—it would be just one day without any suffering." "A place without tears," says the Scripture (Rev. 21:1–4). It's a place where our loved ones have gone, and we should rejoice that they are with God. A cartoonist once pictured a crowd of grieving caterpillars carrying the corpse of a cocoon to its final resting place. The poor, distressed caterpillars, clad in black raiment, were weeping, and all the while the beautiful butterfly fluttered happily above the muck and the mire of the earth, forever freed from its earthly shell. Needless to say, the cartoonist had the average funeral in mind and sought to convey the idea that when our loved ones pass away it is foolish to remember only the cocoon and concentrate our attention on the remains, while forgetting the bright butterfly, our loved one or friend who hovers above us, radiant. That's a great image of heaven.

We talk about this in terms of life after death with the image of the butterfly leaving the cocoon. Even scientists reference this oneness with God in life beyond death. For example, Wernher von Braun once said that he had "essentially scientific" reasons for believing in life after death. He believed that science offers a real surprise for skeptics who think that scientific discovery nullifies religion, because of his knowledge that nothing, even the tiniest particle, vanishes completely. "Science," he explained, "has found that nothing can disappear without a trace. Nature does not know extinction. All it knows is transformation! Now, if God applies this fundamental principle to the most minute and insignificant parts of the universe, doesn't it make sense to assume that God applies it also to the masterpiece of all Creation—the human soul? I think it does."[1] Because of science, not in spite of it, von Braun affirms even more confidently "the continuity of our spiritual existence after death." There is life after death, where in heaven we will be completely at one with God. Is this statement true? Not as a provable fact, but it is true as a declaration of faith. We see now only in "a mirror dimly [or "a glass, darkly," KJV] but then face to face," says Paul in 1 Corinthians 13. Then we will know heaven firsthand.

But Jesus is saying that we don't have to wait until we die to get glimpses of this place, this condition, this state of mind and to experience what we call heaven. We know from the earlier petitions that this first part of the prayer recalls the Kaddish ("Holy") that old Aramaic entreaty that brought the synagogue service to a close. Jesus had surely known it since he was a child.[2]

> Exalted and hallowed be his great name
>   in the world which he created according to his will.
> May he rule his kingdom
>   in your lifetime and in your days and in the lifetime
>   of the whole house of Israel, speedily and soon.
> *And to this, say: Amen.*

Notice the urgency of the last of the prayer—"speedily and soon." Heaven is not something we have to wait for; it's something we can begin to experience here and now. "Thy kingdom come, thy will be done as it is in heaven so also on earth." What is Jesus talking about here? He's talking about a corporate merger, in fact, a corporate takeover, as heaven storms the earth. It's not a hostile takeover, mind you. In fact it's so peaceful and so gradual that many of us aren't even noticing as it happens. Jesus is not just praying that earth be more like heaven, he's proclaiming it as an accomplished fact with his incarnational presence among us. The kingdom of heaven is at hand. In other words, it's coming upon us right here and now. Heaven, says Willimon, isn't just "up there"; it's right here and now. It's wherever we find God with us and ourselves with God. Confucius, who wasn't even a Christian, got it when he said, "Heaven means to be one with God."

Heaven is the place that has a better "culture" than any other you could ever find on earth. We talk about corporations, academic institutions, families, and teams having "cultures." Business-training gurus spend years trying to figure out why the cultures of certain companies are better than others, and then teach them to every budding MBA in sight. Every NFL team is scrambling to figure out why certain other teams have better "cultures" than theirs even though they don't pay the highest salaries for their players. To work in a good culture is like heaven, and to get stuck in a bad one can be a kind of hell. What is a good culture? It's one where people think more about others than they do about themselves. Successful companies think about customers and clients first and the bottom line last. When you take care of your customers in a highly ethical manner, when you do the right thing in the first place, not just to avoid being caught, the bottom line will take care of itself. If, as a teacher, the most important thing to you is that you care that your students learn, then you are going to make sure you are interesting, demanding, and fair, and education will take place at the highest level. When you care about justice issues when it comes to your employees, and when you care about what they think and you know they can help you be even better than you already are, you will ensure stability and loyalty in your organization and everyone else will want to be a part of it. Now, at a very simple level, that's what heaven's culture is like. People get along, they care, and they go the second mile. We don't have to die to go to heaven. We can experience glimpses of it here and now.

Our problem is that we're so caught up in the earthiness of earth. We keep our heads down, hands to the plow, never looking up to see that God wants us to try other possibilities with people who drive us up the wall. God wants us to stop fighting so much, always having to scrap and scrape out our meager little existence here. God wants us to care for the poor when we'd much prefer caring only for ourselves. We know earth's culture all too well. When Will Campbell wrote these words in our time, were they any more shocking than Jesus' were in his day: "We know how it is on earth. It is little warm puppies and the slaughter of seven million Jews. It is Mother Teresa bathing the faces of the dying in Calcutta, and the outrage of Vietnam. It is a little girl trying to extinguish three candles on a birthday cake and succeeding, and a hundred thousand people trying to survive a lightweight bomb in Hiroshima and failing. It is what we call life and it is what we call death. In heaven as on earth."[3]

We are so buried in the day-to-dayness of our earthly existence that we forget completely how it could actually be better, certainly better than it is. Jesus' request for us to pray, "Thy kingdom come, thy will be done, as it is in heaven so also on earth," is a claim that things truly are getting better in our world and our lives because heaven is coming upon us even now. But, not all of us like that, do we? Even during Lent, a penitential season when we try to deny ourselves, we find it hard to give up our little sins. We're not really sure we want "heaven on earth," because it might mean we would have to start being good, and who wants to be all that good?

We've heard that when someone asked the famous revivalist Dwight L. Moody, "Hey, Preacher, can a man chew tobacco and still go to heaven?" Moody replied, "Yes, but he'd have to go to hell to spit!"

We're not so sure we're ready for heaven on earth. Mark Twain once said, "I don't like to commit myself on the subjects of heaven and hell—I have friends in both places!" Nietzsche put it this way: "In heaven all the interesting people are missing." Is that what you believe—that there will be so many Goody Two-shoes in heaven that the whole place will be boring? Not if Martin Luther is there—himself an earthy, rough-hewn, character.

Even Jesus was earthy—calling tax collectors and sinners into ministry, meeting people where they were in their homes or at their parties, but at the same time storming earth with heaven's bright culture.

Jesus didn't go around putting people down, scaring the hell out of people the way John the Baptist did. He wasn't bullying or beating them into the faith, but lifting people up when all they seemed to be was down. Jesus just keeps coming whether we like it or not. Are you a perpetual grump? Jesus is forever storming your life with heaven's joy to cheer you up and make you easier to live with, you old grump. Are you a perpetual worrier, certain that you can keep ships afloat with your worrying? Jesus is forever storming your life telling you to chill. Whatever is holding you back from entering heaven's culture, Jesus is there knocking it down so you can come on in and begin experiencing eternal life.

The trouble is you keep holding back because you're not really sure you want your earth to be as it is in heaven. You're not sure you're ready for all it means. Barth says that in heaven God's will is perfectly done. "Why not among us?"[4] The answer is that we are not positive we can deal with the idea of heaven in our midst. It's too hot to handle. Bob Lively offers a sober reminder in his commentary on this petition when he writes, "Every time we beseech God in seven words requesting that heaven be brought to earth, we're praying for a revolution where love overthrows the long, sad reign of fear and drags the demons of selfishness kicking and screaming into the light of a new day. Consequently, we'd best be certain we mean it before we say, 'on earth as it is in heaven,' because every time we speak these words, we are asking God to turn everything upside down and inside out, including us."[5]

Are we ready for that? Do we really want to change that much? If we want a better world, we do. If we want God's kingdom to come on earth, we do; and if we want God's will to be done and not ours, we do. The only way it's going to happen is when we open our hearts and minds to God's presence among us and to how God intends to use us every day. God reveals Godself in everyone and everything. Our problem is that we don't see God's activity in our midst. We miss it almost every time. The portal to heaven is everywhere; all we have to do is look up and begin seeing the world through "kingdom eyes."

Heaven is here and now. Eternal life is now. When Jesus says, "The kingdom of heaven is at hand," he uses the perfect tense in Greek, which includes past, present, and future. God's presence has been with us from the beginning, is with us now, and will be with us forever. It's more than a state of mind. Milton was only partly right when he wrote, "The mind in itself can make a heaven of hell and a hell of heaven." Certainly your attitude is important. But heaven coming to earth is so much more. It's even more than a lovely mountaintop experience. William Sloane Coffin once described a little piece of heaven in this way: "The Berkshire mountains that fall blazed so with color that Moses would have turned aside at every bush."[6] Don't get me wrong—heaven can be glimpsed in beautiful scenery like that, but it's so much more.

The gate of heaven is everywhere, and God is opening the door to us not only to invite us in, but to work through us to bring heaven on earth. In this way, God's kingdom coming and God's will being done give us hints of the eschatological kingdom to come, one we participate in here and now. Such is the story of Elder Lee, a businessman in Korea, who made a deal with God years ago. If he could be successful in his business, he promised God, he would give something back. He would bring ten thousand people to Christ. When he was successful, very successful in fact, he turned his manufacturing business over to his family and began his search for ten thousand people to bring to Christ. The trouble is, because of the missionaries we sent over to Korea in the mid-1800s, practically everyone in Korea is a Christian, and most are Presbyterians. So he said, "I can't find ten thousand people to convert here." Then he looked at a map of the world and said, "Now, Russia. That's a big country. I'll go there." So he came to Moscow, not knowing the language or anyone, and realized that trying to convert people while walking the streets wasn't going to get very far. Then he thought, "What if I started a seminary, trained pastors and sent them out to convert the ten thousand?" That's exactly what he did. Now, since the early 1990s, he has hired professors who have trained more than a hundred pastors, and Elder Lee has helped them plant and start churches all over the former Soviet Union. Elder Lee is bringing God's kingdom on earth and helping God's will be done "as it is in heaven so also on earth."

Jesus knew exactly what he was talking about as God brings heaven to earth. How? Through you and me.

Questions for Discussion

1. How do you think we can bring today's believers into a deeper understanding of the idea of heaven?
2. Discuss some ways "heaven coming on earth" will change the way you look at your daily life and the ways you will relate to those around you?
3. Name some ways our world seems to bring "hell on earth" instead of heaven, and ideas you have about correcting that problem.

Give Us This Day Our Daily Bread

τὸν ἄρτον ἡμῶν τὸν ἐπιούσιον δὸς ἡμῖν σήμερον

ΤΟΝ ΔΡΤΟΝ ΗΜωΝ ΤΟΝ ΕΠΙΟΥϹΙΟΝ ΔΟϹ ΗΜΙΝ
ϹΗΜΕΡΟΝ

*W*hen I was in Russia lecturing at the Moscow Presbyterian Theological Seminary, one of the other lecturers drew a small circle on the blackboard, then a larger one around it, and then a larger one, all inside a very large circle. He pointed to the smallest circle in the middle, which named the verse for the day. Then he said, "We don't look at this verse by itself. It's in the context of the passage that we're reading, and then we look at that in the context of the whole Gospel, and we look at that in the context of the whole New Testament. Then we look at that in the context of the Old and New Testament, and then the context of the whole Bible." Later I said to him, "That's like a Russian stacking doll, where you have the tiny little doll inside a larger doll and a larger," and he said, "I never thought about it. I'll tell the class next time, and they'll get the point even better that way."

So we look at this one verse in the Lord's Prayer, "Give us this day our daily bread," but we don't look at it by itself. We look at it in the context of the whole of Scripture, especially Exodus 16:1–6 and 13–15, the familiar passage about the Israelites out in the wilderness complaining to Moses that they are starving—if they had only stayed in Egypt, they could have eaten their fill. Moses tells them that God is going to rain bread from heaven, and it will be more than enough. Then come the quails, and in the morning the manna. When the people ask what it is, Moses says to them, "It is the bread which the LORD has given you to eat."

Still understanding the context of this one verse, we move to John 6:25, which follows the feeding of the five thousand story. Jesus has gone to the other side of the sea. When they found him on the other side of the sea, they asked why he had gone to that place. Jesus told them they were looking for him not because they saw signs, but because they ate their fill of the loaves. He reminded them to work not for food that perishes but for food that endures for eternal life. When they asked him what sign he was going to give them so they could see and believe, referring to the miraculous gift to Moses and his people, Jesus told them that it was God who gave Moses the bread and that they should eat this true bread from heaven, which would end their lifelong hungering and thirsting.

As I looked at this verse, "Give us this day our daily bread," I thought this is a very, very simple petition, perhaps the simplest of all in the Lord's Prayer. After all, in the earlier chapters we have been dealing with some pretty elusive stuff. "Our Father who art in heaven, hallowed be thy name. Thy kingdom come, thy will be done as it is in heaven, so also on earth." Now we get this simple phrase, "Give us this day our daily bread." In Greek, it's τὸν ἄρτον ἡμῶν τὸν ἐπιούσιον δὸς ἡμῖν σήμερον: "The bread of the day, give to us today."

George Morrison notes, "Now when you read it unimaginatively, this seems an almost trifling petition. It almost looks like an intruder here. . . . On the one side is the will of God, reaching out into the height of heaven. On the other side are our sins, reaching down into unfathomed depths. And then, between these two infinities, spanning the distance from cherubim to Satan, is 'Give us this day our daily bread.' Our sin runs back to an uncharted past, but in this petition there is no thought of yesterday. The will of God shall be forevermore, but in this petition is no tomorrow."[1] What a seemingly simplistic and narrow entreaty this one appears to be. Yet it's not that simple if you look at it more closely. I see three kinds of breads that Jesus is talking about here.

The first kind of bread is the physical bread that we all need every day just to make it through the day, to live our lives. When we get too hungry, we cry out as babies do, wanting their food, wanting their milk. The Israelites cried out, throughout their travels in the wilderness, "Why did you bring us out here just to starve us? We might as well have stayed in Egypt. We would have been better off." Then God begins to provide, which helps them learn to depend on God. We all need daily bread, every single day. That's what soup kitchens are all about—offering the bread of the world to those who are hungry. When they need it, they need it now.

I remember an experience years ago, on my way to a chapel to officiate at a marriage ceremony. It was time for the wedding to start when a homeless woman with her little baby came up to me and said, "I need milk for my child. My child is hungry. My baby needs some milk."

I said, "Lady, I've got to go do this wedding, which is starting right now. I can't stop to help you now—maybe after the wedding."

"But my baby needs some milk. She needs it right now!"

I looked into the chapel. The mothers had been seated. The groom and all the groomsmen were ready to march in and watch the bride and her bridesmaids parade down the aisle. The organ was playing. I took one more look at the pleading mother's face and held up the whole wedding in order to run to the kitchen, scurrying in my robe, to find some milk. When we are hungry, we need something to eat and we need it now.

So this first bread is this physical bread that finds us with our hands outstretched, reaching up to God for help and for nourishment, and it is God who provides. God is the one who gives us the bread. God, who is the Creator of the universe, is concerned about our daily needs, and stories of the feeding of the five thousand remind us of this over and over again. Jesus is preaching the Word, but the stomachs start grumbling, and they say, "Even if we send out for pizza, we won't have enough for everyone," and Jesus says, "Let's work with what we've got." The loaves and the fish appear, and there's plenty of food for everyone. A good summary of this passage is: You provide the bread, let God take care of the miracle. But what's interesting is that even the bread they provide was first provided by God.

Then later, at the end of the Gospel of John, after his resurrection Jesus says, "Come and have breakfast with me," to his disciples. He has fixed breakfast for them. What does this tell us? It tells us that God Almighty is concerned about us and our daily nourishment, and we see it hidden in this little verse, this "Give us this day our daily bread." The word "daily" here, ἐπιούσιον, *epiousion,* is used only once in the New Testament, and it is here in this place. If you look in other parts of

Greek literature, you find it only in a few little papyrus fragments, and every one where you find it is a shopping list. So here is this shopping list word, *epiousion*, hidden in the greatest prayer of all prayers, the prayer our Lord has given us. Coupled with the feeding of the five thousand and the story of Jesus offering breakfast to the disciples, this little *epiousion* word teaches us that even God Almighty is concerned about lunch! Dale Bruner reminds us that "Jesus was not satisfied when we prayed only for the most important things: God's honor, rule, and will. Jesus felt it important that we give equal time to those matters that some suggest are beneath God's time and trouble,"[2] like bread.

God gives us our daily bread, but also engages us in participating in the production of it, which we see when Jesus asks his disciples to participate in the feeding of the five thousand by producing some loaves and fish themselves.

William Barclay tells about the man in Scotland who had a piece of land that was pretty barren, and he began to try to develop the land, clearing out stones and pulling all the weeds. He nurtured that land until he began to grow vegetables and beautiful flowers. A pious friend of his came by and he said, "Isn't it wonderful what God has done with this bit of ground?" to which the man replied, "Yes, but you should have seen this bit of ground when God had it to himself!"[3] In other words, we are called to participate in God's bounty with our toil. Faith without works is dead. We are called to participate in helping feed ourselves and feed others with the physical bread.

I saw that in Russia, where people needed bread, people who were in poverty, as are many people around the world. On the very last day, at the end of our time of lecturing, I had noticed a man sitting in the back with pastors from all over the former Soviet Union, from Belarus and Moldova and Turkestan and Uzbekistan and Tartistan and Minsk and Crimea—all these pastors and seminary students and one woman, Tatiana, from Siberia. But I noticed this one old gentleman with long hair and maybe only one or two teeth, and with a really rough-looking black suit that looked as if he'd been on the street and a black shirt and clerical collar. His name was Vasily. He was kind of fired up as he listened to us lecture and preach, and then he came up at the end, and he brought each of us who'd been lecturing a loaf of bread. As he presented the loaves to us he also gave us a sermon yelled out in

Russian, which an interpreter translated into English. Later that week, I found out that Vasily had been in the Gulag, or prison, two different times, ten years each, for his beliefs. He had preached the gospel and passed out tracts on the street, and the Communists didn't like it. Here was a real live street preacher, and his ministry today is to bring bread to the homeless under the bridges and to preach the gospel to them. There he was giving us bread, a huge round loaf, which we used in Communion back in the States the very next week.

The first kind of bread we need is the physical bread, the bread that we all need to eat, but then there is a second, a spiritual bread, the bread that we share around the Lord's Table. It is the mystical bread. It's not just a memory, a mere memorial, as Zwingli thought. It is the mystical presence of Christ, who is with us and who wants to come into our lives and change our lives and help us be better than we are.

I remember serving stew at our church soup kitchen and seeing one of the homeless men who had a kind of faraway look, a sort of sad look, in his eyes; he hadn't even eaten much of his food from the first round. I said, "There are seconds," and he said, "No, thanks, food won't solve what my problems are." Buechner says that some kinds of emptiness are so great that not even the blue plate special can touch them. And Buttrick says that when we pray, "Give us this day our daily bread," we are not praying to some celestial flour merchant in heaven who provides only physical bread. We are praying to the Lord of the universe, who provides us spiritual bread, the bread that lasts forever that Jesus talks about in the Gospel according to John. It is the bread that you and I share in when we read the Scripture every day and when we pray every day. It is the bread of heaven that nurtures our souls. If we stay away from the Scripture too long, our souls shrivel up. They atrophy. It is the bread of spirituality that we receive in sermons and in Sunday school lessons and in small-group ministries with prayer groups and circles and studies of the Bible.

I used to feel bad when people couldn't remember my sermon from a few weeks before, and then I realized I can't even remember what I preached last week, and it wasn't a big deal because it didn't matter whether people remembered sermons. What matters is whether or not they are nourished. How many of you remember the meals you had last week? How many remember what you had for lunch on Wednesday or on Monday? How many of you remember any meal that you've had? Maybe in France, a wonderful feast on that one last night you were there, at that little crêperie—maybe you remember that one. But we rarely remember anything else. Still, we know whether or not we've been nourished and fed, and the same is true of the spiritual bread that we experience every day and every week.

This spiritual bread changes lives, and I saw that in Russia. I witnessed firsthand the huge revival that is going on there. It's unbelievable, seeing the changed lives. Let me just give you two examples. As we flew from Moscow to Perm in the middle of the night, they kept the lights on in the plane and served us salmon. It was as if it were daytime, and we arrived at 5:30 in the morning. We were met by pastors who took us on up to Lys'va.

One of the pastors was a gentleman named Ivan, and another one was a gentleman named Viktor. Viktor we met in Lys'va, and he was a pastor in another town nearby. Now Viktor, prior to perestroika, was a dyed-in-the-wool Communist. He was one who had even looked around and checked on people if they weren't communist enough. When he had gone on a trip with others from his chemical plant to the United Kingdom, he would check on everyone to make sure none of them ran away or did things they weren't supposed to do. He was also an alcoholic, and he was having serious marital problems; his wife was ready to divorce him. Then his daughter, following perestroika, went to one of the Pentecostal churches that was starting up, and she converted to Christianity, which caused Viktor great consternation. Then his wife converted, but he didn't know it because she never told him. She was planning to divorce him and leave him, so to her it didn't make any difference whether she told him she'd converted or not. She was going to go her own way, because he was so much of a party-loyal Communist and did not want to give up drinking. But he got mad about his daughter being converted, so he said, "I want to go to church with you and see what this is all about." He went to church and was converted himself. He didn't say anything about it at work, but his coworkers started noticing that he wasn't drinking as much. In fact, they put notches on the window in between the times he was drinking and they noticed it was a month at a time, and then sometimes two months at a time. His wife also noticed the difference, and decided to give their marriage another try. Then he came to this seminary in Moscow, and now he is a pastor, bringing others to Christ. Such is the transforming power of this spiritual bread.

Then there was Ivan, an enormous young man who was an expert in wrestling, judo, and karate, and I found out as we were talking with some others in the group that he was a former Russian Mafia chief. He had his own Mafia gang. I was anxious to hear his story, which he finally revealed through an interpreter. His job as a Russian Mafia chief was to be an enforcer when people did not pay their bribes or do what the Mafia wanted them to do. It was eerie being around him. I imagine his congregation gives him no trouble at all. How did he make the transition from godfather to pastor? I was curious to know. Here is how it happened: His girlfriend was converted by a Pentecostal Presbyterian pastor—an odd combination of words, to be sure—and Ivan got mad. He wanted to find out what was going on. "I'm going to the service with you tonight and I'm going to beat the hell out of this preacher." When they got to the service, there were eight hundred people there. He said, "Dang, I'm good, but not this good! I'll wait until the end of the service to beat the hell out of the preacher." So he sat through the whole service, and instead God "beat the hell" out of him, and he was converted to Christianity by the power of the risen Christ. Like the apostle Paul, who was a murderer and a persecutor of Christians, Ivan was knocked flat himself by the one they call Jesus and then decided to go to seminary. Now he is a pastor in a small town in the Ural Mountains. Such is the power of the spiritual bread to change lives, to create *metanoia*, to cause repentance to occur, no matter who you are.

When I was preaching in one church with Sergei Petrov translating, I was talking about how exercise is good for you, and real runners tell you that "when you get used to running, then you begin to like it." Sergei translated it and everybody began laughing; then he smiled, trying to explain something to them in Russian. I said, "What's going on?" He replied, "The word for running is *bic*. By accident, instead of translating your phrase, 'When you get used to running,' I said the word for God, which is *bog,* in place of the word for running, so it came out 'When you get used to God, you begin to like it.'" In fact, that's what they heard, and in fact that's what is happening to those people. They are "getting used to God" in Russia, and it is the spiritual bread that is transforming lives.

But then there is the third bread, a final bread, and that is global bread. All you have to do is travel around the world, and you begin to see it. You can travel to France or Scotland or India or South Africa or Mexico or Korea or Russia, and you begin to see how global this bread is, because we do not pray, in the first petition, "*My* father who art in heaven." We do not pray, "Give *me* this day, *my* daily bread." We pray, "Give *us* this day, *our* daily bread." And when we truly believe that God wants us to be together, it is God who breaks down the barriers between us.

One night I was leading a Bible study with Russian military officers—colonels, majors, captains, getting ready for the big Army Day celebration the next day. It was an incredible experience. It was a Tuesday night. The big celebration was Wednesday. And I said to them, "I never imagined that I would be standing before you, teaching you the Bible." I was teaching them the Lord's Prayer in Greek. They were learning it quickly, because their alphabet is so close to the Greek alphabet, and they loved it. We talked about the Lord's Prayer and its meaning for their lives as soldiers. At the end of the session, they said to me and to others, "Pray for us." Their names were Sergei and Vadim and Vidaly and Nicolai and Yefgheni and Alexi and Yuri and Viktor, and they said, "Pray for us, and we will pray for you."

God is the one who breaks down the barriers between us. Such is the power of this global, eschatological bread. Joan Gaines, another pastor from the United States, stood before these Russian military officers and said, "When I was a little girl in California, in Sacramento, in the 1950s, we had bomb drills, nuclear bomb drills, because Mather Air Force Base was just twenty miles away, and we knew it was on the first strike list. We would have these drills where they would pull heavy, dark curtains across the big windows, and we would go to the wall and we would cover our faces and cover our eyes, just to practice, making sure the blast would not blind us. Then one day when I was eight years old, I went to my mother and I said, 'I want to write the President of Russia. And I want to write him a letter and say, *Americans are nice people and you Russians are nice people. Why can't we just figure out how to get along?'* And my mother said, 'The President of Russia will never get this letter, but what you should do is pray that God will someday bring us together.'" Joan continued, "Now here I am speaking to Russian military officers. Here I am, preaching the gospel to Russians, and God has brought us together."

When we flew in to Perm', the pastors brought us around to show us defunct ballistic missiles that are not used anymore. They pointed and said, "That one, New York in twelve minutes; that one, Washington, DC, fifteen minutes. But we are not using these now. You are the first Americans to come to this city, because it was off limits, because this was a city that would shoot the missiles off, but now we are here together, and it is God who brings us together."

It is God who is doing great things around the world. There is a great awakening occurring all over the globe. It is happening in Asia, in Africa, in South America. Now it is happening in Russia. We will see missionaries being sent to the United States and Europe from these other places because that's where the church is growing by leaps and bounds. With our brothers and sisters in Russia, South Africa, Korea, China, and India, it is God who is giving us little glimpses of that eschatological bread of heaven that we will all share someday when we sit down at the marriage supper of the Lamb in heaven, the symbol of the peace and harmony that can happen in our time.

How important it is to remember how the story ends! Such was the dilemma presented by a visiting preacher who looked out and noticed everyone was asleep, so he decided he would do something to shock them and wake them up. So he said this sentence in the middle of the sermon, "I have spent the best years of my life in the arms of another woman who is not my wife," and the entire congregation woke up suddenly, and then he went on to say, "And it was my mother." Everyone was relieved. There was another preacher in that congregation, who the next Sunday, when he got up to preach in his own church and saw everyone was asleep, decided that he would do the same thing. And he said, "I spent the best years of my life in the arms of another woman who was not my wife," and the whole congregation was shocked, and then he forgot how the story ended and said, "But for the life of me, I can't remember her name." How important it is to remember the end of the story! The end of the story is the eschatological bread, which

God wants us to share, the eschatological bread that brings us together with one Lord, one faith, one baptism, one God and Father of us all.

Questions for Discussion

1. Discuss Jesus' line that humans "shall not live by bread alone," and its meaning in the context of this petition in the Lord's Prayer.
2. How are you involved in bringing physical bread to the world's poor and hungry? How could you get more involved?
3. Is it possible that sometimes we in the church get so involved feeding people's stomachs that we forget to feed their souls? How can we do both without making people pray and do Bible study before we feed them?
4. In what ways could you be experiencing more fully the global and eschatological bread of Jesus Christ around the world?

Forgive Us Our Debts/Trespasses/Sins

καὶ ἄφες ἡμῖν τὰ ὀφειλήματα ἡμῶν
ὡς καὶ ἡμεῖς ἀφήκαμεν τοῖς ὀφειλέταις ἡμῶν

ΚΔΙ ΔΦΕϹ ΗΜΙΝ ΤΔ ΟΦΕΙΛΗΜΔΤΔ ΗΜѠΝ
ѠϹ ΚΔΙ ΗΜΕΙϹ ΔΦΗΚΔΜΕΝ ΤΟΙϹ ΟΦΕΙΛΕΤΔΙϹ ΗΜѠΝ

*T*he great thing about Christianity is that it's so easy. You come to church. Bring your sins, dump them on God, sing "Amazing grace, how sweet the sound, that saved a wretch like me," get forgiven, and go home a new person altogether. Now, tell me, what could be better than that? This is really easy, right?

Wrong.

One of the hardest things in the world is to accept the fact that we really are forgiven. Preachers stand before us every Sunday and offer the declaration of pardon: "In Jesus Christ, you are forgiven." But who among us really believes it? Paul Tillich says the hardest thing in the world for us to do is to accept the fact that God accepts us and is ready for us to move on with our lives. Yet we still pray it in the Lord's Prayer, hoping that maybe this time we'll get the point as we pray these famous words once again, "Forgive us our debts, as we also have forgiven our debtors." We come to church week after week and try our best to say it with confidence.

"Forgive us our sins"—this is the way some seminaries say it in order to be inclusive and avoid the debts/trespasses debate. One meaning for the word for forgive here is "to let go of" and the other is "to cancel," as in the sense of canceling, remitting, or pardoning of all debts. We all know that "debts" is a Jewish figure of speech for sins, and when you get right down to it there's not a lot of difference between debts, trespasses, and sins, because in every case it means our failure in duty, our moral and spiritual bankruptcy in what we owe God and others around us, our treading on other people's feelings, space, and territory. But we do say it differently in different denominations, don't we, and we all notice this. When I was a parish pastor, every time I performed a wedding where there were lots of guests, I always knew we had allowed into the building a whole crowd of Methodists or Episcopalians when we came to the Lord's Prayer. When we get to this phrase, Presbyterians say "debts" then have to wait as all the Wesleyans rush through their "trespssessessess. . . ." The same happens at funerals. Once, before a memorial service, I came into the back of the chapel at Sparkman Funeral Home and the organist was just playing along the way they do—funeral home organists can play anything with their eyes closed or while turning and talking to you at the same time. This one was no different; she just kept on playing as I told her about the service. When I told her that the soloist would be singing the Lord's Prayer, without missing a beat she asked, "Methodist or Presbyterian?"

What's the difference anyway, and what difference does it make? Well, there's the urban legend and then the real story. The urban legend goes like this: The Scots were merchants, and the English were landowners. To sin against a Scot meant that you hadn't paid your debts, so Presbyterians and others within the Reformed tradition prefer "debts" in the Lord's Prayer. On the other hand, the English, being landowners, believed that the chief sin was trespassing on their property—thus their preference for "trespasses" in the Lord's Prayer. It sounds good on the surface but probably isn't worth the paper on which it's printed. After all, it's an urban legend.

The more reliable explanation goes like this: Thomas Cranmer, who wrote the Book of Common Prayer, the prime liturgical source for Anglicans, Episcopalians, and United Methodists, followed Tyndale's version of the Lord's Prayer, which incorrectly translates ὀφειλήματα (*opheilemata*) as "trespasses," when the word for trespasses is actually παραπτώματα (*paraptomata*), which appears two verses later in verse 14, after the end of the Lord's Prayer. The Scots, however, followed the King James Version, which correctly translates *opheilemata* as "debts." This accounts for the difference between Reformed communities and Anglican-based communities when it comes to this verse. But, really, does it make all that much difference? Whatever way you translate it, it means that you've wronged someone and are in trouble for it. That may be one reason that new translations say, "Forgive us our sins" (as in Luke 11:4), which gathers in both debts and trespasses and is a win/win or a lose/lose for everyone, depending on how you look at it.

Remember also when we pray, "Forgive us our debts/trespasses/sins as we forgive others theirs," that we are not only praying for our own debts/trespasses/sins but those of the whole world. After all, this is the communal prayer, the OUR Father, which gathers us all in. Saying the Lord's Prayer is not done in a private confessional booth, but within community. Even when we are by ourselves, as prisoners often are, we still say this prayer in the context of the large body of believers, even if it is only in our minds. Helmut Thielicke makes this point when he says, "In these words we bring to the Father the whole mountainous burden of sin that weighs upon the whole world and like a nightmare haunts this present historical hour."[1]

We didn't need Reinhold Niebuhr to tell us. We can turn on the news and see for ourselves. We look in the mirror and around our own house. Eden's damage is everywhere. Original sin taints everyone, even the saints among us, especially the ones who keep bucking for a vacancy in a stained-glass window. As Henry Ward Beecher once said, "I don't need John Calvin to tell me about total depravity, I have my congregation to show me that!" And lest clergy think they are immune, remember that there are three fingers pointing back every time we point one out from a pulpit. Despite the fact that we church folk see ourselves as pretty decent people, living basically good and upright lives, we know when we're honest that we are not much better than the next person, no matter how hard we try. Oh, we think we are better than the town drunk, but we aren't, because our sin is the sin of pride, one of the worst of all. It puts us in company with the Pharisees. Some of us might find it offensive to pray that we are "miserable offenders," as in the confession from the old *Book of Common Prayer*, because we have done our best to be "good" all week. As Everett Fullam notes, "People often pray that prayer with a condescending tolerance that allows them to think inwardly, 'I'm praying this along with those people who really need it.'"[2]

The truth is we all need it. We need to be reminded of that every single day we stand before the judgment seat of God in need of God's redeeming grace, because no matter how hard we try we cannot overcome our shortcomings on our own. We need extra help. So says Oswald Hoffmann: "God is not the problem. We are. Here is something most of us do not like to admit. We are debtors to the goodness and grace of God. Our debt is not just one solitary failure. We have debts, many of them. We feel the weight of our debts only when we put them on the scale of God's grace and goodness toward us."[3]

The idea presented in the Lord's Prayer is that we owe everybody something, especially God. So what does God do? God says, "From now on, all debts are canceled, thanks to the redeeming work of Jesus Christ in both cross and resurrection." In other words, in Jesus Christ, God tears up all our IOUs. They are erased from the memory bank, which is something we can't do on our own. Try as we may, we cannot erase the imprint of human sin. It's a stain that will not go away through our own effort.

When I was in high school I used to peek out the window when my sister, who was two years younger, would come home from a date and sit out in a car in the driveway with a boyfriend, doing whatever they did out there. Being a somewhat nosy, overprotective big brother, I would glance out the window to see what was happening, of course, and to make sure she was all right. One night I couldn't get a very good view from my window, so I went around to her room, leaned over her desk, and, straining in the dark to see what was going on, stuck my hand in a still slightly damp picture she had painted that afternoon. There was no way to touch up that painting or explain my way out of the big handprint I'd left right in the middle of it. Like Lady Macbeth, I said, "Out, damned spot!" but try as I might there was no way to erase the print of human sin that continually mars God's picture of how our lives can and should be. The reality is, no one can erase our mistakes but God.

But there's good news! As we pray, "forgive us our debts," Jesus reminds us that God has already erased the memory banks on our debts and we don't owe anything anymore. Once a wealthy English businessman who lived on the Continent was driving a Rolls Royce he had owned for years. Going down a bumpy road, he hit a deep pothole and broke an axle. When he shipped it to England, it came right back repaired, with no bill for the work. He knew the warranty had run out, so he asked why there was no charge. The reply from the company was, "We have thoroughly searched our files and find no record of a Rolls Royce axle ever breaking. Thus you owe nothing."

Our problem is that the rear axles of our lives are always breaking down. But because of Christ record of it keeps getting erased from God's memory banks, and God keeps fixing us up. We wait for the bill, but keep finding out that we owe God nothing, nothing at all. "You mean nothing for that awful thing I did back there, Lord? To think I've been tithing all these years to pay for that! I owe you nothing for that? You know, Lord, which thing I mean. To think I gave big-time to the last capital campaign to cover that! You mean it's all free? There's got to be a catch somewhere." All debts canceled, all sins pardoned. Just let it all go. If it's that easy, why don't more people cash in on Christianity and live happier lives? Karl Menninger of the Menninger Clinic once said that if he could convince the patients in his psychiatric hospitals that their sins really are forgiven, 75 percent of them could walk out the door the next day.

But, we just can't believe it. Here is the human race weighed down with the burden of sin, unable to accept the fact that with God all debts are canceled, that we are, in Ernie Campbell's words, "locked in a room with open doors."[4] The fact that we can't get up and walk out of the Menninger Clinic or break out of the cycle of our own depression is our own doing, not God's. With God the doors have always been open, debts always canceled, trespasses erased, and sins forgiven.

Maybe that's the trouble with Christianity. It's just too easy. We sin, God forgives, we sing a hymn and go our way. There has to be a catch here somewhere. Sure enough, there is. It's like a tiny string attached, not God's but ours. The string is this: you have to be willing to accept God's forgiveness, but you'll never be able to accept it until you can first forgive others who have done you wrong or failed you in one way or another. Forgive us our debts as we forgive our debtors.

Jesus thought this point was so important that, of all the petitions in the Lord's Prayer, this is the only one he repeated bluntly right after the prayer. You can almost hear him saying, "For yours is the kingdom, the power, and the glory. Amen. But there's one more thing I want to say—a kind of footnote, if you will. As to this idea about forgiveness, I want to make sure you get the point. If you forgive others their trespasses [and here the word "trespasses" is actually used], your Heavenly Father will also forgive you; but if you do not forgive others, neither will your Father forgive you." Now there's a hook that will get your attention.

He brings it up again in Matthew 18 with the call to forgive about seventy times seven, and the debtor whose debt was canceled but who tried to squeeze the guy below him. This point about us forgiving others before receiving God's forgiveness is a very troubling one, since it catches all of us sooner or later. Does it include the scoundrel who cheated us once and the spouse or child or parent who never listens or communicates? I have to forgive them before I receive God's forgiveness? Yes. You mean the rapist and the murderer? Oh, well, they're easy to forgive until they hurt you or your own family. Them too, Lord? Yes. You mean bosses who are unfair and loved ones who hurt us? What about the people who committed those awful atrocities on 9/11? The answer is, "Yes, yes, a thousand times yes." For when you can forgive even your worst enemy, it is evidence that the regenerative grace of God is transforming your life, and as you are being transformed you are becoming more and more open to God's love and forgiveness for you. This is not a law so much as the natural outpouring of a sincere soul who understands that the more we want God's will to be done in our lives, the more conscious we are of our shortcomings. The more conscious we are of our own shortcomings, the more forgiving we are of the faults of others, even when they have done us harm. The ultimate example, of course, is Jesus on the cross, who says, "Father, forgive them, for they know not what they do."

During the Christmas season in 1983, a photograph from Rome flashed around the world. Picture it now—the corner of a sparse prison cell with radiator below and bars on the windows above. Two men sit close together, knees almost touching, on molded-plastic chairs, one in a white cassock, white cape, white skullcap, the other in a blue crew-neck sweater, jeans, blue-and-white running shoes from which the laces have been removed. *Time* magazine described the startling scene with these words:

Last week, in an extraordinary moment of grace, the violence in St. Peter's Square was transformed. In a bare, white-walled cell in Rome's Rehibba prison, John Paul tenderly held the hand that had held the gun that was meant to kill him. For 21 minutes, the Pope sat with his would-be assassin, Mehmet Ali Agca. The two talked softly. Once or twice Agca laughed. The Pope forgave him for the shooting. At the end of the meeting, Agca either kissed the Pope's ring or pressed the Pope's hand to his forehead in a Moslem gesture of respect.

We'll never know—what did they talk about? When questioned while emerging from the cell the Pope replied, "That will have to remain a secret between him and me. I spoke to him as a brother whom I have pardoned, and who has my complete trust."[5]

Such is the power of the grace of God. I know what you're thinking. That's easy for the Pope to say. After all, he's the Pope. Besides, there's a difference between forgiving and forgetting. "Forgive and forget," we say. "Let bygones be bygones." But are they the same? Can we really, say the Jews, forget six million killed in the Holocaust? According to Elie Wiesel, to forget is to commit a crime against justice and memory; to forget is to be the executioner's accomplice. Forgiving is one thing, forgetting is another. If you forget, history may be doomed to repeat itself. Besides, forgetting is not all that easy. Frederick Buechner is right: To forgive somebody is to say one way or another, "You have done something unspeakable, and by all rights I should call it quits between us. However, although I make no guarantees that I will be able to forget what you've done and though we may both carry the scars for life, I refuse to let it stand between us. I still want you to be my friend."[6]

Perhaps God is the only one who can ever completely forgive and forget, since it's so hard for us to do both. In 1981 King Juan Carlos and Queen Sofia boycotted the wedding of Prince Charles and Lady Diana to continue a protest that dates back to 1704, when Gibraltar became a British colony. The monks at St. Catherine's Monastery are still mad at Konstantin von Tischendorf for stealing Codex Sinaiticus (the oldest manuscript of the Bible) from them in the mid–1800s. Some things are just hard to forget! Like a deep hurt between spouses, friends, parents, and children. Perhaps we will never forget them, but we can forgive them, because if we don't—if we don't make peace with those around us, we'll never be able to make our peace with God. That's why Jesus has us pray, "Forgive us our debts *as* we also have forgiven our debtors" (italics added). *As* we forgive others, so God will forgive us. If we refuse to forgive others, we will never truly experience the grace of God ourselves.

So don't pray this prayer unless you are ready to forgive others who have wronged you; for what you are praying literally is "Forgive me, God, the way I'm forgiving others." But if you aren't forgiving others, if you aren't letting all that stuff they have done to you go, you are cutting yourself off from the love of God, not because of God's doing, but because of your own actions. This is not conditional forgiveness, for God's forgiveness is not contingent on our forgiving others. God will never hold back. We're the ones holding back. We wall ourselves off from God's giving love when we don't share that love with others. Someone once told a pastor, "I never forgive!" to which the pastor replied, "Then, sir, I hope you never sin." Archbishop Temple reminds us that though it is often said that Jesus promised we would be forgiven if we repent, the reality is he said we would be forgiven if we forgive.[7]

Bob Lively puts it poignantly when he writes, "As citizens of this present moment, God is inviting us to forgive *liberally.* For if we hope to remain where we've traveled thus far with Jesus, we must stretch ourselves in the very direction we ask God to stretch for us. Simply put, we must forgive. Realistically we cannot expect to forget moments of personal injury. We may repress them, but we never forget them. Nevertheless, we must make grace the norm of 'on earth as it is in heaven.'"[8] How can we make forgiveness the norm of our present lives if we won't forgive others for wronging us?

If we continue to boil in anger and resentment, it will actually affect our health, since we now know scientifically that anger and resentment create an unhealthy stress that consumes vitamins and minerals and suppresses the immune system. Wouldn't it be nice if anger and resentment and the inability to forgive would consume fat cells instead of vitamins and minerals? If that were the way things worked, we would all be trim and fit. Instead, anger leads to stress and stress can actually make us physically and emotionally ill, and thus unable to experience the washing, cleansing grace of God, which is in fact the healthiest thing we will ever know this side of eternity. Think about what salvation means. The Greek word for it is σωτηρία (*soteria*), which is translated *health, wholeness, peace, harmony, oneness,* and *shalom.*

Prison chaplain Pierre Raphael summarizes beautifully the meaning of this petition in the Lord's Prayer when he writes: "We are born imperfect, with a marked attraction for tumbling into the abyss. And yet the unfathomable plan of heaven is that we be reborn and become children of God. To do this, an understanding of our guilt is needed—indeed is precious. We realize we are journeying to God with the burden of our sins. We have remorse. Repeated misdeeds anesthetize us; we cannot clearly see our wounds. God's forgiveness is so passionately offered that Christianity might be summed up in four words: the religion of pardon."[9] He goes on to say, "Forgiveness is a celebration." What Raphael is describing here is the overflowing, unmerited love of God. It's a love we need every day of our lives. We are as dependent on this love as we are on the bread we prayed for in the previous petition. In fact, we could just as well pray this one this way: "Give us this day our daily love as we daily give it to others," for a day without God's love is a day without warmth or light.

What is this love of God? It's a love that never counts or keeps track. It's an extravagant love that forgives seventy times seven, a love that makes no sense and leaves no room for grudges or revenge. It's a love that cancels all debts, forgives all trespasses, erases all sins, and says, "Today, Lord, and from this day forward, I let it all go into your loving hands." It's a love that allows a father or a mother to forgive the enemy who killed their child in war. It's a love that will not let us go, a love that writes on every gravestone the one-word epitaph that is on a man's headstone in upper New York State. What is that one word? "Forgiven."

Through Christ, God has written that word on your heart and mine. *Forgiven. Forgiven. Forgiven.* So also we must forgive others. When we can and when we do, we will truly know what it is to pray and to live, "Forgive us our debts as we also have forgiven our debtors."

Questions for Discussion

1. Think about people who have wronged you in some way or other. You haven't forgotten—perhaps you never will. But have you forgiven them for what they did? If not, why not?
2. Think of ways you have hurt others and need to tell them you are sorry, in order to cleanse your soul. What is it going to take for you to be able to apologize?
3. Have you ever completely accepted the fact that God forgives you for all the awful things you have done in your life? If you haven't, do you think it might have something to do with your forgiving those who have wronged you?
4. Resolve now to let old vengeances and angers go so you can, with God's help, move on with your life.

9

Lead Us Not into Temptation

καὶ μὴ εἰσενέγκῃς ἡμᾶς εἰς πειρασμόν

ΚϪΙ ΜΗ ΕΙΟΕΝΕΓΚΗС ΗΜϪϹ ΕΙС ΠΕΙΡϪϹΜΟΝ

I wonder how many of us would just as soon skip over this little verse, tucked as it is toward the end of the Lord's Prayer.
Wouldn't it be great if we could revel a little longer in the glory
of God's forgiveness? "Amazing grace, how sweet the sound,
that saved a wretch like me!" But Jesus knows all too well how
quickly we slip back into our old ways. Just because we have
been forgiven and have even forgiven those who have wronged
us doesn't mean that we are going to stay on the right track the
rest of our lives. Patterns of behavior are never changed that easily. Anyone who has tried to change a golf or tennis swing knows
that. A new way of doing things has to be "grooved" into the system by daily repetition. Practice makes perfect, as long as it's
perfect practice. In fact, the day we turn our lives over to God
and promise to be different is only the first day of a long journey back to God. The edge of the road back is slippery and the
road is full of potholes and obstacles. There are all sorts of siren
songs and alluring entertainments alongside the road, which dis-
tract us from our true path. Jesus understands this because he
himself was tempted and tested along the way. So he adds this
tight little phrase immediately after the one on forgiveness as a
gentle reminder: "Lead us not into temptation."

For perspective on this petition, it's important first to look at
a couple of passages that give us some background. We begin
with the first chapter of the Letter of James, verses 2–4, 12–16
(NRSV). "My brothers and sisters, whenever you face trials [or
tests] of any kind, consider it nothing but joy, because you know

that the testing of your faith produces endurance; and let endurance
have its full effect, so that you may be mature and complete, lacking
in nothing. . . . Blessed is anyone who endures temptation. Such a one
has stood the test and will receive the crown of life that the Lord has
promised to those who love him. No one, when tempted, should say,
'I am being tempted by God'; for God cannot be tempted by evil and
he himself tempts no one. But one is tempted by one's own desire,
being lured and enticed by it; then, when that desire has conceived, it
gives birth to sin, and that sin, when it is fully grown, gives birth to
death. Do not be deceived, my beloved." From James we move to
Hebrews 2:18. "Because he himself was tested by what he suffered,
he is able to help those who are being tested" (NRSV). Notice that the
word for "test" is the same word in Greek as for "tempt" (*peirazo*);
so you will hear them used interchangeably. In fact, the New English
Bible translates this verse, "Do not bring us to the test."

My Grandpa Carl was more of a doer than a talker, but when he did
talk everyone listened. He always had little witticisms that he loved to
share, especially with those of us who were younger. I remember many
times walking around on his twenty-acre property on the edge of Tulsa,
Oklahoma, when I was a little boy, and he would share these little
words of wisdom, like "A job worth doing is worth doing well," and
"Don't look a gift horse in the mouth," and "Don't ride a willing horse
to death." One day he said, "Little ships stay close to shore while big-
ger ships can venture more." By this, he meant children should keep
quiet around adults. I noticed he said it frequently when I was around.
I would always ask lots of questions like "Why is this?" "Why is that?"
"Why, why, why?" The grownups would always say, "Because. Quit
asking so many questions." Then one day my grandfather paused for
dramatic effect and made this stunning but simple statement: "Bill, it's
easier to stay out of trouble than it is to get out of trouble." There is a
lot of wisdom in that line that could serve as a whole chapter in a book
on business ethics. In essence, that is what Jesus is saying in his petition "Lead us not into temptation."

A little boy scrambles up on the kitchen counter even though he
knows he's not supposed to get near the cookie jar. But his mother is
not around, so he dives into the cookies. When his mother walks in
unexpectedly, he's got chocolate chips all over his face. She says,

"What are you doing?" and he replies, "I was just going up to smell them, and my tooth got caught." Sounds like Adam and Eve trying to hide in the bushes and trees of the garden after tasting the forbidden fruit. "It's easier to stay out of trouble than to get out of trouble." The problem is we don't believe it, or maybe we just don't want to hear it. We mean more here than when the friend of a dieter hides the chocolate cake or puts on the refrigerator door a sign that reads, "Lead us not into temptation"; more than when the friend or loved one of an alcoholic hides the bottle. It's about trying to avoid in the first place awkward situations that get you into trouble. "Lead us not into temptation."

I remember how during seminary I served as a hospital chaplain in Louisville General Hospital. I loved pulling emergency room duty because there was so much excitement. There was always something going on. There was nothing boring about being in the emergency room, especially on Derby Day in Louisville, Kentucky. On Saturday night of Derby Day one year, the emergency room was packed with people who had been shot, stabbed, beaten, and maimed, you name it. All kinds of things were going on. I remember as if it were yesterday walking with the coroner into a darkened room to tell a family that their teenage son had been shot in the head at close range. As a very young man, I felt completely helpless trying to share with those stunned parents the news of their young son's death. I'll never forget one of them saying, amidst all the weeping and sobbing, "What was he doing in that part of town?" What indeed? "It's easier to stay out of trouble than it is to get out of trouble." Just ask Martha Stewart or the leaders of Enron. I remember asking Jeb Stuart Magruder, a student of mine at Princeton Seminary, about Watergate and all that went on there in the White House. When I asked him, "How did you all get so far, so deep into this? How did Haldeman, Ehrlichman, John Dean, and all of you get so caught up in this?" Magruder replied, "Bill, you don't know what it's like to be in the White House. The power and the glory make you think that you can do anything you want."

"It's easier to stay out of trouble than it is to get out of trouble."

"Lead us not into temptation."

My Grandmother Correy had another saying, which seems to apply here: "When in doubt, don't." In other words, if you have to think about it too long, it's probably wrong. Your own internal conscience will ring the moral and ethical bells. But the problem is we get so used to walking the gray line of ambiguity, so deaf to the moral and ethical bells ringing in our heads, that we don't even question our actions anymore. We become so immune to "everybody's doing it" that we suddenly realize, usually too late, that we have crossed the line and there's no turning back. We get so accustomed to this immoral way of doing things, even though in our heart of hearts we know it's wrong, that we rationalize the cheating and lying because, if we don't do it, we'll lose the rat race. Then one day we wake up to the realization that we may be winning the rat race but we are still one of the rats.

"Lead us not into temptation." "When in doubt, don't." It's easier said than done.

Helmut Thielicke reminds us that it's not just the little sins and peccadilloes of children snitching candy or the cheating on our income tax. There's a deeper, subterranean temptation that is bringing us down, and that is the temptation to be separated from God. We find ourselves caught up in this so easily in the world in which we live right now.[1] With TV, radio, the Internet and entertainment of all sorts coming at us hard and fast, it's difficult to stop and just sit and think about God, to think about the question of God, to think about the question of eternity. How hard it is to find time to do that!

Peter Whybrow's book *American Mania: When More Is Not Enough,*[2] helps us understand that Americans today are living lives addictively turbocharged by the brain's pleasure centers, which put us in daily pursuit of status and possessions, the things that turn away the very people who will bring us happiness. He says that consumption, this idea that we need and we want more and more than we can ever get, activates the neurotransmitter dopamine, which rewards us with pleasure. It travels along the same brain pathways as the drugs caffeine and cocaine. We are so caught up in it in our society that Whybrow is not sure where it's all heading, but it's not a good place, because we often find the more and more we get, the less and less happy we are.

When a bicycle was stolen from our family's garage, I remember feeling violated, as if someone had invaded my privacy and taken a part of me. Then I wondered, how could I have become so attached to an inanimate object? I realized that I had bought into the postmodern concept that my belongings define my existence. In other words, we are what we own. How sad and pathetic! Those who lost everything in Hurricane Katrina had to redefine their existence and start over. Not that I'm ready to dump everything and become a hermit. The joys of poverty are highly overrated. On the other hand, if you think you can buy happiness by acquiring more and more, you are in for a big surprise. "Lead us, O Lord, not into the temptation of thinking our possessions define who we are. Whatever separates us from God, lead us away from that, O Lord."

Of course, we want to ask immediately, "Why would God ever lead us into temptation in the first place?" In fact, if you go back to James, right toward the beginning in verse 13 (NRSV), he says, "No one, when tempted, should say, 'I am being tempted by God,'" because God would never tempt anyone. No one is tempted except by one's own desire (James 1:13–14 NRSV). That's where the temptation comes from. "God is not the enemy," writes Oswald Hoffmann. God is "not forever trying to trick people into making a misstep."[3] So God won't tempt us, but God does test us. That's the other meaning of this word *peirasmon*. It means trial or test, and it also means temptation. So it's not that the temptation and the testing make us into greater sinners. Testing can actually make you a better person.

Earlier James says to count it a joy that you experience various trials, because these trials, these tests, lead to endurance and steadfastness, and steadfastness leads to maturity and completeness, "lacking in nothing." So rejoice in your testing because testing can be good. But if testing is good, why does Jesus say, "Lead us *not* into testing, lead us *not* into temptation"? I and many other scholars think that what Jesus is really saying here is, "Lead us not into more testing than we can handle." You know how those airline pilots getting trained to fly big planes go through all kinds of testing before they are licensed. They are tested on flight simulators, and the first ones are simpler and a little bit easier to handle, and then when they've passed that, they move to more difficult ones, then they move to catastrophic situations. If they were thrown by the trainer into the catastrophic situations too early, they wouldn't be able to handle them. So God gives us the testing that we can handle. "Lead us not into more testing than we can handle," we say to God, and God then gives us all kinds of testing, in interesting kinds of ways.

But the most difficult testing is when we are tested and challenged to give up what we treasure the most. That's the hardest one of all. In great novels and movies, the characters who are the most three-dimensional usually don't have choices to make between good and evil. Those are too easy. The choices are usually between this good and that good, and it's hard to figure out which way to go. Thus God tests us, asking us to choose what we treasure the most in order to show our loyalty to God. So Abraham is asked to give up Isaac, to give up his only begotten son, his precious son, the one that God promised to him who would bring a great nation out of Abraham. All the nations will come out of Abraham, and now God is asking Abraham to give up his son. Yet he is ready to do it. You don't know how much he agonizes—he must have agonized—but the Scripture says nothing about his agony. The Scripture simply has Abraham saying, "Yes, I will obey." And just as he is about to sacrifice his own son, the Lord sees that he is faithful, loyal, and obedient, and the angel provides the lamb in the thicket.

Think about Jesus, ready to give up what he treasures the most, even when he is tempted out there in the wilderness. Imagine, here is a man who with every fiber of his being wants to alleviate suffering, and finds that he will be able to end hunger completely, end poverty, if he just turns his life away from God and over to Satan. He gives up what he could treasure the most, satisfying people who are hungry, by turning to God, by giving his loyalty to God. What a difficult decision that must have been.

Sometimes we are tested in that way. So we pray, "Lord, lead us not into more testing than we can handle; but we know that sometimes you are testing us when asking us to give up what we treasure the most." We pray it when we sing "A Mighty Fortress Is Our God." In that great *Ein' Feste Burg*, by Martin Luther, we sing, "Let goods and kindred go, this mortal life also." We are singing that we are ready to give up everything to follow God. "Lead us, O Lord, not into more testing than we can handle. Lead us not, O Lord, into too much testing."

Sometimes when God tests us, God tests us at the very point of our greatest strength. Have you noticed that sometimes your greatest strength can, when it's pushed too far, become also your greatest weakness? God does sometimes test us at this point of greatest strength.

When he was a boy, Napoleon wrote an essay on the dangers of ambition, but it was his own ambition that wrecked his life and his career. Moses was known for his meekness, and yet in an impetuous way, when he didn't trust God, he turned and struck the rock, and because of that was not able to go into the promised land. Peter, who was known for his impulsive courage, at the very point that he could profess faith in Christ denied Christ three times. God often tests us at the point of our greatest strength, and sometimes we want to say, "God, I've had all the testing that I can handle. No more testing, God. It's just enough. I can't take any more."

I remember when I was going through seminary and then was a candidate for ministry, we used to be examined extensively on the floor of our presbytery. Now, when a candidate is examined before a presbytery, that candidate may get a couple of questions and then gets passed through for ordination. But back in the day, a long time ago, when we used to go for sometimes two or three hours, they could ask you any question they wanted to. They could ask about theology or church history or Bible—anything from the Bible, Hebrew, Greek, philosophy, it didn't matter. Systematic theology, philosophical theology—they could ask you any question they wanted from the floor. And at the end of one of these three-hour exams, when a student was just totally exhausted, an elder stood up on the back row and said to him, "Young man, I have one more question: Would you be willing to go to hell for the glory of God?" He answered, "Sir, I'd be willing for this whole presbytery to go to hell for the glory of God."

Sometimes we want to say, "God, I can't take any more testing. I've had enough." That's what Israel finally said, and God heard Israel and humanity's cry, and God sent God's only-begotten son to stand the ultimate test on the cross for you and for me, that we might have life.

There is now a final way we can look at this very simple phrase, "Lead us not into temptation." Lead us not into more testing than we can handle. So often, when we look at it we look at it sort of negatively: keep us away from the bad things. But in reality there's a positive side to this. What we are saying is, "Lord, lead us in the paths of truth and peace and joy and harmony. Lead us in the direction you want us to go with our lives so that we are not anxious, we are not worrying, we are not so upset about the littlest thing, the smallest thing that happens to us. Bring us into your pathway, O Lord. Show me the way, O Lord." So there is a positive side to "Lead us not into temptation."

Thielicke, describing a young man who daily battled his temptations with every fiber of his being, points out that the young man's perennial preoccupation with them only increased his involvement and assured his repetitive surrender to them. Instead, Jesus wants us to be positive and turn to him and his supportive force field of protection against everything in life that would drag us down. "There is," writes Thielicke, "a sense in which we can say that we should not fight against temptation, since this only mires us more deeply. We should rather keep our eyes on the Lord."[4] Someone once asked a counterfeit expert how he identified the false coins and bills. "Do you spend a lot of time looking at counterfeits?" "No," replied the expert, "I spend a lot of time looking at the real thing."

I remember, years ago, a woman named Marguerite Mizell, who had spent a lifetime in the mission field, telling me that when she was eighty-seven she went in for a physical and the doctor said, "Marguerite, you're just as healthy as can be. You're going to live to be ninety-seven." When she turned ninety-seven she said to her doctor, "Now what?" And he replied, "Well, Marguerite, I guess it's in the Lord's hands now," and in the Lord's hands she lived another four years. What Jesus is trying to tell us in the Lord's Prayer is that, whether we're seven or ninety-seven, it's all in the Lord's hands. That's what we mean when we say, "O Lord, lead us not into temptation. Lead us in your way of truth and peace."

Questions for Discussion

1. Look back on your life and think of key moments when life has tested you. How did you handle those various tests that came your way? Did they break your spirit and discourage you or make you a better person? Discuss.

2. How do you handle the temptations that come your way? Do you have an appropriate moral antenna for recognizing them and avoiding them, or do you find temptation a daily struggle you cannot confront without God's help?

3. Do you think support groups that deal with certain temptations are helpful? If so, which ones?
4. Can you think of times in your life when God gave you more tests and trials than you could handle? If so, how did you deal with it?

Deliver Us from Evil

ἀλλὰ ῥῦσαι ἡμᾶς ἀπὸ τοῦ πονηροῦ

ⲀⲖⲖⲀ ⲢⲨⳭⲀⲒ ⲎⲘⲀⳭ ⲀⲠⲞ ⲦⲞⲨ ⲠⲞⲚⲎⲢⲞⲨ

*T*here was a very spiritual woman who would step out on her porch every day, raise her arms to the sky, and yell, "Praise the Lord!" One day an atheist bought the house next door. He became irritated with this woman's public display of spirituality and after a month of her yelling, "Praise the Lord," the atheist went out on his porch and yelled back, "There is no Lord!" But that did not deter her. One cold, wintry day, when the woman couldn't get to the store, she went out on her porch, raised her hands, and said, "Help me, Lord, I have no more money, it's cold, and I have no more food." The next morning, she went outside and there were three bags of food on the porch, enough to last her a week. "Praise the Lord, you have saved my life!" she yelled. The atheist stepped from behind the bushes and laughed, "Woman, you are a fool. There is no Lord. I bought those groceries!" The woman looked to the heavens and said, "Praise the Lord, you sent me groceries and you got the devil to pay for them!" Deliver us from evil and get evil to pay the tab. "Deliver us from evil." What an interesting and odd way for the Jesus Prayer to end!

First of all, let us be clear about what this phrase says and doesn't say. Jesus is not saying here, "Deliver us from suffering," although on some occasions that is an appropriate prayer, because we all suffer at one time or another. When our loved ones are dying and we realize there is no way to turn things around, our prayer is certainly, "Deliver us from suffering." I'm sure that is the prayer of Dr. Richard Olney, the California neurologist and renowned expert on ALS who now has ALS himself. That's right: the man who has written more than fifty scientific papers on the subject and founded the ALS Center at the University of California, San Francisco, now has the very disease he has been studying most of his life. So the headline in one newspaper article on him was "Long-time Expert on A.L.S. Now Knows It All Too Well."[1] "Deliver us from suffering. O Lord, deliver us now."

We all pray that prayer at one time or another for ourselves or our loved ones and friends. But that's not the entreaty Jesus has in mind here at the end of the Lord's Prayer. Perhaps Jesus didn't ask us to pray, "Deliver us from suffering," because he knew even he himself was about to suffer. Never mind that he was the Son of God, which you'd think would normally get you special privilege, or at least a pass from pain and agony. Even though Scripture records him as giving it a try when in the Garden of Gethsemane, he prays, "Father, if it be possible, let this cup of suffering pass from me. Yet not my will but thine be done." Jesus knows we can pray, "Deliver us from suffering," and sometimes, in God's will, we are delivered, but not always. In fact, Paul says we should "rejoice in our sufferings, knowing that suffering produces endurance, and endurance produces character, and character produces hope, and hope does not disappoint us" (Rom. 5:3–5). Thus, because suffering often teaches us something about ourselves, Jesus does not have us pray, "Deliver us from suffering."

Instead, he has us pray, "Deliver us from evil." Literally, this means deliver us from the evil one. Use whatever name you like—Satan, Diabolos, the Tempter, the Liar, the Murderer, and the Cheat. Whatever you want to call it, it's something palpable in our world that is lurking not just in the shadows of dark alleys, but in the most attractive and alluring places, sometimes among the most clever and persuasive people. The evil one is God's adversary, the one who is constantly trying to throw us off our game. Beelzebub is not just a red hairy figure with pitchfork and horns—something like that would be too easy to spot. No, the evil one is the palpable force of malice in the world, which constantly attacks anything essentially good and offers charming invitations to turn to the dark side. It may be a personal force or, says Barclay, "what we might call the cumulative effect of all the evil acts and evil

decisions which have been part of the human scene."[2] Whatever the
case, it is there just outside your door or there looking back at you from
your television or your computer, there next to you whispering in your
ear. It's what turns us all into Scott Peck's "people of the lie."[3]

This petition, "Deliver us from evil," and the previous one, "Lead
us not into temptation," offer counterbalances to our normal ways of
thinking and acting by calling on God to help us in the fight against
evil that seeks every day to corrupt our lives. We pray this prayer hon-
estly and sincerely, because we know that God has made us free spirits with free will and, because of that, sometimes we slip and fall.
Sometimes we make wrong choices and go the wrong way in our
lives. Deliver us from the evil we participate in daily. Deliver us from
the evil we promote and propagate ourselves.

Of course, part of our problem is that we allow the world to define
reality for us. We go with the world's description of the way things
are. Part of the message of this petition is that reality is not what we
think it is. As a result, the Bible is constantly countercultural in its
description of things. Think how countercultural it is in a world that
says, "There is no God," to announce that God is the Creator, the
Redeemer, and the Sovereign Lord over all nature and history. Think
how many times you see something like that in the media's description of the way things are.

We know that language shapes reality. The world is named for us—
"light," "ball," "Mommy." If you get the wrong language or you hear
the wrong story, you don't really understand how things are and how
they can and should be. Language and story tell us who we are; they
not only help shape our worldview, our *weltanschauung*, but they
shape and form our identity. For example, the Hopi Indians have a
totally verbal language. As a result, everything is in process in their
worldview. One does not talk to them about the creation as a point in
time when God created the world. God is constantly in the process of
creating, every single moment. Thus, though Einstein's theory of relativity can cause problems for Western culture with our noun-oriented
language, the Hopi Indians heard Einstein's theory and said, "That
makes perfect sense." In other words, one's language helps shape
one's view of reality. In the same way, "story" helps fashion the lens
through which we see the world.

If whole segments of history are deleted from our knowledge base, as they were in Russia during the twentieth century or as they were with blacks and women in this country for a time, people aren't sure who they are or where they fit in. "Who defines reality, anyway?" asks Will Willimon. "Through what metaphors and images will we describe the world? In any given week, something like fifty million Americans attend a service of worship in their church, whereas only a small fraction of that number go to a movie. Yet when you read this morning's newspaper or watch morning television, there will be no mention of church. Most of the talk is of movies and movie stars, leading one to believe that Hollywood is more important than Jerusalem. In a way, the powers make it so—our lives are in the grip of the images that the media offer us."[4] Don't get me wrong. Jesus is not preaching an "Against Culture" position, where religious people name everything about the world as bad and retreat from it totally, burying their heads in the sand. I like going to the movies as much as the next person. But I refuse to allow what I see or hear there define the reality with which I live my life. There are destructive and negative sides to Hollywood as there are on Wall Street and Main Street. The same is true with television evangelists. But that doesn't mean everything in the world or in TV religion is bad. What this petition, "Deliver us from evil," says, as did the previous one, "Lead us not into temptation," is this: "God, give us the wisdom to discern the good from the bad and the courage to change what needs to be changed."

What the Gospel writers were doing was renaming the world in the light of the Christ event. They kept saying, "The world wants you to believe this is the way things are, that you are no good, that your life is nothing unless you step all over anyone who gets in your way, that your life is nothing unless you satiate every hedonistic desire that comes your way. But Jesus is here to tell you that there is another way." Thus we pray, "Show us, please." And Jesus replies, "Pray then like this: Deliver us from the evil that pulls us down!"

"Deliver us from evil" means in part "deliver us from any theodicy that turns a blind eye to injustice, oppression, and abuse in our society or seeks to justify it as simply part of life that we can't do anything about." In her commentary on Maximilian Kolbe's witness in Auschwitz, Susan Nelson reminds us that we can do something about evil even when we succumb to it. Father Kolbe, a priest who had been imprisoned as part of the Holocaust, took the place of a condemned man in the starvation cell. He continued offering support and encouragement to his fellow prisoners until the prison physician administered that lethal injection that ended his life, and was later beatified for his acts of mercy. Nelson suggests that Kolbe's witness emboldened other inmates as the story of his action spread throughout the camp, and thus muted the grip of terror that made that place such a living hell. Nelson concludes, "As one who chose to die in an act of compassion, Kolbe thus revealed that evil, while not defeated, could be defied—thus subverting the Nazi intent to destroy any sense of dignity and hope in the prisoners."[5]

The biblical writers demonstrated vividly in the stories of Jesus' Palm Sunday entry, with all its false and empty praise, how it finally ends with the passion, where Jesus takes on evil firsthand. Thus Passion Sunday points to the decisive skirmish and atoning victory to come. Our problem is that we don't catch what's really going on. We keep forgetting that Jesus has already gone head to head with evil and won the battle for us. We forget all that in the party atmosphere of the palm branches. Over and over again we succumb to the seductive power of evil, which eventually leads to a kind of spiritual death. Gardiner Day puts it this way: "Spiritual death means estrangement from God which is Hell. Cut off from God, our spirits wither." He goes on to illustrate his point, imagining a young man who has done something so terrible that his family has disowned him. As far as his family is concerned he does not exist. They don't talk to him or e-mail him, and they won't return any of his calls. Until he turns like the prodigal and says he's sorry, as far as he is concerned he feels as if he is in a kind of hell, completely cut off from the people he loves.[6] But the fact is, no one loves you more than God, the one who formed you in your mother's womb, the one who has watched over you all your life, the one who lifts you up when all you seem to be is down. Yet, when we turn away from God for whatever reason, when we break the commandments, when we do things we know are wrong, it's not so much that we're going to hell as that we feel as if we're already there. So when we pray this petition, "Deliver us from evil," we're really praying, "Lord, deliver me from the hell I'm in right now."

We pray it fervently and frequently, because no matter how much we try to get out of the hell we sometimes find ourselves in, eventually we realize we can't, not on our own. We pray, "Deliver us from evil," because we can't deliver ourselves, no matter how hard we try. Once while on sabbatical from teaching, I served as interim pastor of a church in Richmond, Virginia. During that year a woman sent me a card that on the front showed a cartoonlike picture of a long-haired, bearded man in a burlap sack, the kind you'd see in Herald Square in Manhattan or in Speakers' Corner in Hyde Park in London. He is holding a sign that reads, "You must pay for your sins!" Now, that's a fine card to send your pastor. Inside it read, "If you have already paid, please disregard this notice." If I have already paid? Of course I have already paid, but not through my own effort—only through the redemptive power of Jesus Christ. On our own, we cannot overcome evil, no matter how hard we try.

Our battle with demonic malevolence is a cosmic, eschatological struggle, and only Christ can deliver us from this insidious evil. Only Christ can, to use Barth's language, "snatch us from the jaws" of psychic defeat. Before Christus Victor, the evil one is an "idiot," a "scarecrow," a "nonentity."[7] Thus, when Christ "delivers us from evil," people are literally "saved for new life."

The positive side of "Deliver us from evil" is the fact that Christ helps us set up "systems of goodness." Think about it in terms of young people, who continually represent the future hope of our world. The National Study of Youth and Religion, the most comprehensive research study ever done on faith and adolescence, revealed that devout teens are more likely than others to do well in school, feel good about themselves, stay away from sex, drugs, and alcohol, and care about the poor. According to this study, religion helps foster healthier, more engaged young people who live more productive and hopeful lives.[8] A church in Texas has for years been working with less-privileged children to give them confidence, strong values, training for more responsible lives, and scholarships to college. One such young Hispanic woman who had grown up attending the program once remarked to her pastor, "I've made an anecdotal observation about Saturday School. All the young people in my neighborhood who have been through Saturday School are the ones who are still in school, making good grades, not into drugs or teenage pregnancy and are going on to college, and all the young people who haven't been through Saturday School are the ones who are dropping out and ending up in jail." The pastor replied, "Gracious, we're saving lives!" You never know how your one good deed or one good word can help deliver others from evil.

But who inspires us to deliver others from evil? Would we do it on our own? I don't think so. Christ is the inspiration. Because of him and his atoning work on our behalf, we know that evil will never have the final word. So writes Schnackenburg, "Because the prayer is offered in the faith that God's kingdom is coming, fear of the power of evil is eliminated." In other words, prayer to God means trusting that God "is stronger than the evil powers of destruction and annihilation."[9] There are three things to remember about God when you are in trouble: (1) God loves you all your days; (2) God knows more about your situation than you will ever know; and (3) God sees where your life is heading. No matter how deep and far down you go, God will go with you, God is there.

How do we know God is there when we descend into hell? We know it by what happens to Jesus on Palm/Passion Sunday. Jesus goes right into the teeth of evil as he heads into Jerusalem, first by facing evil head-on, then by succumbing to its terrible fury on the cross on our behalf. Then he takes on evil by conquering it in both death and resurrection. Finally, he moves us toward his eschatological future, where Eden's damage and evil's illusory power are ultimately overcome, and in so doing he truly does "deliver us from evil" from this time forth and forevermore.

Questions for Discussion

1. Do you think the modern avoidance of referring to Satan as a person causes contemporary Christians to think that evil is not a force to be reckoned with in our time? Discuss.
2. In your opinion, how prevalent in today's world is the Manichaean idea that God and evil are equal forces battling it

out on some cosmic Star Wars–like stage? How does this contemporary view influence your understanding of "Deliver us from evil"?

3. Why is it so hard for individuals and groups ever to see themselves as participating personally or corporately in evil in our time? Why is it so much easier for us to see evil in others than in ourselves?

4. How do today's self-help techniques feed into the idea that we can deliver ourselves from evil and thus do not need to pray this petition at all? Discuss.

11

For Thine Is the Kingdom

ὅτι σοῦ ἐστιν ἡ βασιλεία καὶ ἡ δύναμις καὶ ἡ δόξα εἰς τοὺς αἰῶνας

OTI COΥ ECTIN H BⲀCIⲀEIⲀ KⲀI H ⲀΥNⲀMIC KⲀI H ⲀOZⲀ EIC TOΥC ⲀIⲰNⲀC

*O*ne Sunday morning, an elderly woman walked into a local country church. The friendly usher greeted her at the door, "Good morning, ma'am. Where would you like to sit?"

"The front row, please," she replied.

The usher said, "You don't want to do that. We have a visiting preacher today who is really boring."

The woman bristling at the comment, asked, "Do you know who I am?"

The usher said, "No, ma'am, who are you?"

She replied, "I am the preacher's mother!"

The usher asked, "Do you know who I am?"

She said, "No."

He said, "Good."

Some people come to church Easter morning as anonymous Christians, not wanting anyone to know who they are. Unlike the preacher's mother in this story, they don't want to troop down to the front row of the church. Instead, like the usher, they would just as soon keep their identity a secret. That's what you call an anonymous Christian. Sometimes people hide their identity as Christians even on Easter, because they are afraid of what their friends or coworkers might think. They wouldn't want to get caught going to church. Or maybe they hide their identity because they think others will ridicule them or make fun of them, as some did during the time of the early church. Think about

/ 85

Peter, Mr. Have-Sermon-Will-Travel himself, who got weak-kneed when confronted that awe-filled night when Jesus was brought before the high priest and ended up denying Christ. "Do you know who I am?" "No," said the soldier. "Good," said Peter. Imagine that first Easter, when it was dangerous to believe in Jesus, who had been condemned and crucified as a common criminal. No wonder they could hardly believe it. Look at the end of the Gospel of Mark: "And they said nothing to any one, for they were afraid." The end of the resurrection story in Luke has the men saying they didn't believe the women's story because they thought it was an idle tale. Because of religious persecution during the Communist era, Christians in Russia had to keep their beliefs to themselves for most of the twentieth century. They knew exactly what the early Christians had suffered. What does this lead to? A muted and tentative faith that cannot express itself openly and fully, the same kind of cautious and subdued faith we see in Europe and the United States, both of which celebrate more secular societies.

You almost get that tentative feel when you read the conclusion of the Lord's Prayer as we have it in its original form. It ends with "Deliver us from evil. Amen." What kind of ending is that? After all they had been through, the early church people knew intuitively that the Jesus Prayer needed something more. They knew something had happened, something so remarkable that not only had their little lives changed but the whole world had been transformed dramatically. The resurrection represented a cosmic paradigm shift, a "tipping point," so cataclysmic and so mystical that they knew the carpenter's prayer needed a stronger finish. So they added a footnote, and what a footnote it is, for it is a peroration of praise that sings with a swelling rhythm of poetic beauty: "For thine is the kingdom and the power and the glory, forever. Amen." There is certainly nothing timid about that! It sounds a lot like the "Hallelujah Chorus" in Handel's *Messiah*. This little footnote allows the Jesus prayer to crescendo to the end with certainty, the certainty of the resurrection. The Galilean carpenter had crafted a beautiful prayer and the church he had set in motion, through the inspiration of the Holy Spirit, had beautified it more.

Often we close letters and e-mails with "Sincerely," or "All the best," but Gerhard Ebeling notes that those are little salutations that tell more about us than they do about the one to whom the letter is addressed. The difference with this prayer is that its ending tells us more about God than it does about us.[1] It's a conclusion that voices confidence in the present and the future because it understands who is in charge and in whose presence we live all our lives.

Maybe you are a seeker trying to figure out what Christianity is all about. Maybe you are just starting out in the faith and you're not sure what you believe or why you are even interested in learning more about God. Maybe you are a longtime Christian, but your faith has been scarred by some bad religion along the way, and you're not sure you believe any of it anymore. You're stuck in church on Sundays hoping no one will ask you your name. Well, guess what? This last phrase in the Lord's Prayer is for you, because it not only affirms God, it affirms you wherever you are in your life right now and says, "You don't have to hide anymore!" After all, God is in charge and because of that your life has meaning and purpose, you have a place, and you know what it is. That's the meaning of "For thine is the kingdom and the power and the glory, forever. Amen."

The people in the early church certainly believed it, and therefore inserted this phrase at the end of the Lord's Prayer. They added it because God had added something to Jesus' life called the resurrection, which we celebrate with confidence no matter what else is going on in the world. The early Christians were good Jews, and they knew that all synagogue prayers ended with an ascription of praise to God. Think of David's blessing in 1 Chronicles 29:10–11a (NRSV), following the offerings at the time of the building of the Temple, "Blessed are you, O LORD, the God of ancestor Israel, forever and ever. Yours, O LORD, are the greatness, the power, the glory, the victory, and the majesty; for all that is in the heavens and on the earth is yours." In other words, this little phrase, "Thine is the kingdom and the power and the glory," was simply a familiar liturgical response like those they had heard in the synagogue. The worshiping congregation was simply responding to the celebrant, as Christians around the world do every week in the liturgy when the leader says, "Praise the Lord!" and the congregation responds, "The Lord's name be praised!" Or "The Lord be with you," "And also with you." Joachim Jeremias reminds us how "in Judaism prayers were often concluded with a 'seal,' a sentence of praise," often extemporaneously uttered by the one who was praying.[2]

This last phrase is in reality little more than a footnote. I was looking at someone's PhD dissertation recently and noted that there were 362 footnotes for only 318 pages. Think of the huge role footnotes play in all scholarly documents. They round them out and put the final touches on them in order to make them complete. The same is true in the Bible. At every turn you run into this footnote or that one at the bottom of the text, explaining another Hebrew or Greek meaning for a certain word or verse. Suddenly the reader says, "Oh, now I see, that's what that means!" For some people, footnotes are merely an afterthought, while for others they are crucial to grasping the truer meaning of the text. Such is the case with this little footnote, "Thine is the kingdom and the power and the glory, forever. Amen."

There is no new information being imparted in this climax of praise at the end of the Lord's Prayer. Even though Jesus didn't say it, he could have, because it harmonizes what he has been saying throughout this great prayer. This doxology is more of a summary of where we have been and where we are going. In fact, it's a synopsis of what Easter is all about. For on that day of all days in the Christian year we say loudly, boldly, and confidently to the whole world that the kingdom, the power, and the glory of our lives belong to God. In other words, in life and in death we belong to God—all that we have and are find confident hope in the providence of a sovereign and loving God.

Earlier we explored the meaning of "kingdom" when we dealt with the phrase, "Thy kingdom come." We know that it is not a place so much as a condition, a way of life, and what it calls for is an act of submission to God. I pledge allegiance to God above all other allegiances including my country, which is why the cross always stands above the flag for Christians. I pledge allegiance to the risen Christ, who was dead as a doornail but now walks among us. I pledge allegiance to the Christ in you, the hope of glory. To pray, "Thine is the kingdom," is to say, "I surrender to you, O God, all my rival kingdoms and turn my life completely over to you."

What is the early church saying here by adding this doxological phrase to end of the carpenter's prayer? It is saying that Jesus is right there in your midst because the stone has been rolled away, and through his resurrection he is bringing his kingdom on earth. His kingdom is in your midst, and he is right there in front of you ready to lead you into places of joy and new life you have never seen before. He is ready to break down the barriers between you and those people you thought were your enemies. That's what I saw in Russia as I led Bible studies and prayed with Russian military officers in Moscow who said to me, "Now we are friends in Christ. Thank you for coming from America to share the gospel of Jesus Christ with us." This was a sentence I never imagined I would hear in my lifetime. Such is the true kingdom that the Sovereign Lord is bringing on earth—"as in heaven, so also on earth." To pray, "Thine is the kingdom," is to believe that God is truly sovereign over all nature and history, and live our lives accordingly.

But here's the catch—God's kingdom is recognized only by those who see Jesus in their midst. Pilate couldn't see it because he was looking at it from the wrong place. As Helmut Thielicke reminds us, it's like those stained-glass windows in your church. If you go outside the church, the windows appear to you as only gray monochrome. There is no way to tell whether they are fine works of art or merely soot-covered windows that need to be cleaned. But the minute you enter the church, "the windows begin to shine and the whole story of salvation, captured in brilliant color, rises up before you." In other words, the mystery of God's kingdom can be perceived and comprehended only when we are actually "in" it.[3] While trying to decipher a letter from a fellow Christian written in Russian, I realized that I had translated the whole thing except for one word. Try as I might, I could not find it in any Russian dictionary at my disposal. So I asked a Russian friend named Igor, who looked at the letter and smiled broadly. "What?" I said, obviously frustrated. He replied, "Dr. Carl, you say this word all the time." "What?" I replied, exasperated. "It's 'Jesus'!" he laughed. It was right there in front of me. Jesus was there all the time, and I just kept missing him.

Open your eyes and you can see the kingdom. Open your hearts and you can experience the power. To pray, "Thine is the power," is to recognize that all our powers pale in contrast to the power of God. For only God has the power to create, to redeem, and to heal. The word for power here is δύναμις (*dynamis*), which gets translated into English as dynamite! We talk of hearing a dynamite speaker or seeing a dynamite movie. To the early Christians the resurrection was dynamite, which means it was fueled by the power of God. God has the power to create, the power to heal, and the power to redeem. God's power is explosive and transforming, able to turn confusion into clarity and sorrow into joy. Our own meager power pales in comparison to the power of God.

The trouble is the power of God isn't always there when we need it, even in the church. Sometimes you wake up in the morning and you just don't feel the power of God is with you. After worship one morning, a woman standing at the door said to her pastor, "That was a good sermon this morning." When the pastor replied, "Don't thank me; thank the Lord," she retorted, "No, it wasn't that good!" Sometimes it seems as if the power of God isn't with you. But when it is with you, then you can accomplish more than you ever imagined. That's what happened that first Easter morning. Those earliest of Christians said, "We're not afraid of the Romans who persecuted us and put us down. We're going to share this gospel wherever we go." So this little Jesus movement, which should have died out, took off and spread around the world, and the apostle Paul said, "I'm not afraid. I'm not going to hold my identity as a Christian behind my back any more." Later Constantine said, "I'm going to bring it up from below ground. We're not going to persecute these Christians any more." And Augustine and Aquinas said, "We're going to put the structure and the form on this theology so the whole world will comprehend it." Then Luther and Calvin stirred Europe, as Knox transformed Scotland, and Wesley and Whitefield and Edwards ignited the faith in America in that Great Awakening. I believe there is another great awakening occurring now in Asia, Africa, and South America and also in Russia. The power of God is something that only God can provide. It is the power of undiscourageable love. The most we can do is to share in that power.

When we share in that power we also share in the glory of God and pray with all our hearts, "Thine is the glory." We only share in the glory because the glory of God is intrinsic to God, as intrinsic to God as light is to the sun and as blue is to the sky. You don't make the sun light; it is light. You don't make water wet, it is wet. Nothing we can ever do will ever change that. So also the glory of God revealed in the resurrection. The glory of God is intrinsic to God.

But glory is not intrinsic to us. You can take a CEO, strip her of all her power and fine clothes, give her only rags to wear, leave her on the streets for a few weeks, then stand her next to a homeless person, and you won't be able to tell the difference. Why? Because her glory is not intrinsic to her. It is granted to her by someone else. Strip us down to the bare essentials and we are all the same, with no glory to our name. All we can do is share in the glory of God. And that's what we do every Easter.

Sharing in the glory means sharing in the victory and rejoicing in that victory. That's what this final phrase of the Lord's Prayer is. It's a loud shout of joy as we share vicariously in the victory of Christ over sin and death. We understand this. When defeat comes to a football or basketball team it casts a pall over a whole city or state, the way the cross cast a shadow over Golgotha and the disciples' little Palm Sunday parade, and the way death and divorce can cast a shadow over a whole family.

But victory! Victory lifts us an extra inch off the floor. When your team wins, the one you throw your allegiance to, it makes you feel important. To share vicariously in a victory is to give your life a whole new lift. That's exactly what the early Christians did. They shared in the victory of Jesus Christ on Easter morning. If we share in the glory, we ought to show it. The Russian Christians in Lis'va, up in the Ural Mountains, prayed and sang with their hands in the air. Their belief was "If we share in the glory, we ought to show it," if not with hands upraised, at least with a glow on our faces and a new joy in our hearts. Believers like this know what it means to be "in the zone," in other words, in *kairos* time more than *chronos* time. They understand the true meaning of "forever" at the end of this prayer, because life lived fully in God's realm of glory is life that has lost all sense of time, life that never worries about the past, the present, or the future because it is life that is full of joy and peace and harmony. It is life governed by incarnational time. "When the time had fully come," says Paul in Galatians 4, God sent the Son to redeem us and bring upon earth divine kingdom, power, and glory. No wonder Christians around the world smile and rejoice when they finally understand the truest meaning of this famous footnote.

That's what the early church did on that first Easter morning, and that's what we ought to do every day as we pray this trumpet burst of praise: "Thine is the kingdom and the power and the glory from this time forth and forevermore. Amen."

To God be the glory!

Questions for Discussion

1. If Asian, African, Russian, and Latin American Christians are participating in the worldwide explosion of the faith that is occurring at the dawn of the twenty-first century, why are so many European and American Christians still timid about expressing their faith openly?
2. Does it bother you that Jesus never said the closing phrase of the prayer that we say liturgically? How does it affect your view of the Lord's Prayer, knowing that the early church added this phrase later? Discuss whether you think it was a good addition or whether they should have left it as Jesus presented it in the first place.
3. In what ways does this closing petition help you rethink how you look at the ideas of kingdom, power, and glory in our world today? Explain.
4. Discuss the difference the word "forever" makes at the end of this prayer, and how it influences the way you live your life.

Amen

Ἀμήν

ⲀⲘⲎⲚ

A preacher in a very traditional church, where proper decorum was regularly observed, was halfway through his Sunday morning sermon when someone in the congregation yelled out, "Amen!" The preacher nearly fainted. Once he regained his composure, he cleared his throat and continued. For a second time the man yelled, "Amen!" This time the preacher glared at him. By now the entire congregation was awake, wondering what would happen next. The preacher paused, then plowed on into his sermon once more. When the man yelled, "Amen!" even louder than the first two times, the preacher said to him from the pulpit, "We don't do that in our church." "But I've got religion!" said the man with enthusiasm. "Well," replied the preacher, "you obviously didn't get it here!"

What does it mean when we say, "Amen," during a sermon or at the end of a prayer? It means, "I agree." That is what we do at the end of the Lord's Prayer. We come to the end with a resounding affirmation for everything that has gone before. It is the end of the prayer, but for believers it is really the beginning.

Jesus has taught his disciples not only how to pray but exactly what to say in proper prayer. Furthermore, his liturgical tutelage has spanned not only nations and races but generations of believers, for two thousand years. Like the disciples, finally now at the end of the prayer we are just beginning to catch what he has been saying all along. So we say, "Amen!" to put an exclamation point on this, the most beautiful of prayers. We do so with reverence, respect, and complete comprehension of the consequences. Why? Because to say, "Amen," in a haphazard or flippant fashion to assertions we do not grasp is to risk trampling on sacred ground. Amen-ing is not trivial business. To "Amen" someone is to offer the nod of affirmation, a nod that will accompany appropriate behavior changes in lifestyle and relationships. In other words, there are consequences to saying, "Amen."

In Deuteronomy 27, Moses says that the Levites are to inform all the people they shall be cursed for making a graven image, dishonoring mother or father, moving their neighbors' stones, leading the blind astray, withholding justice from the stranger, the orphan, and the widow. After each admonition, Moses declares, "And all the people shall say, 'Amen.'" In Hebrew it's אָמֵן, which means "Yes, I agree. I get it and affirm it." Think how universal this word is. We see it in the Hebrew Bible. In Arabic it's آمِين ʼĀmīn, which is found at the end of prayers in the Koran. Instead of translating it, the Gospel writers simply adopted it and passed it on, to the point that it was used widely in liturgical settings throughout the early church. Since its root in Hebrew has nuances of faith and belief and points to strengthening and encouragement, we see how seriously the ancients took this word. To say "Amen" and mean it was to turn all of one's life over to God. It meant agreeing with every fiber of your being.

We are not talking about hair-shirt, chest-beating concurrence that went on for hours. In fact, if you look carefully at Jesus' sermons, teachings, and prayers you are struck immediately by their sheer brevity. The same is true at the end of the famous Jesus Prayer. This is no sevenfold "Amen," no protracted conclusion to Handel's *Messiah*. Not with Jesus. He believed that succinctness was close to Godliness. He made his point and stopped. Luther's homiletical advice was, "Stand up, speak up, and know when to shut up." E. B. White and Will Strunk's lecture on brevity in their *Elements of Style* was simply, "Be brief, be brief, be brief." Jesus got to the point quickly, then watched to see the reaction. What is our reaction to this most ancient and yet contemporary of prayers? Are we ready to say the "Amen" with all our strength, demonstrating our verification that the blessing is true and our hope that the prayer will be answered? If we are not, we have missed the point.

To say "Amen" is to say, "May it be so." May what be so? The answer is, everything that Jesus has been trying to teach us in this great prayer. May it be so in your life and mine. May it be so for both rich and poor. May it be so in every part of the world. May it be so for all time and eternity.

What a resounding end to this simple but profoundly moving prayer! Saying your "Amen" to it, says James Mulholland, is like standing with your bride or groom, "before God and these witnesses," saying "I do" and "I will" to the wedding questions, then repeating your vows.[1] It's a two-way street. Even as you are vowing to hallow God's name, watch for God's kingdom coming and God's will being done here on earth as it happens in heaven and forgiving others their sins against you, so God is vowing to sustain you with daily bread, to forgive you, to lead you away from temptation and deliver you from the slavery of sin in which evil ensnares you. But saying our vows is the easy part. The hard part is living up to them, just as in a marriage.

The day you get married had better be a day of confidence. It's the day you affirm, "This is who I am in relationship to the other, and this is how I plan to act for the rest of my life." Saying "Amen" at the end of the Jesus Prayer is like that. Barth, Luther, and the Heidelberg Catechism all agree. "Prayer," writes Barth, "is not an undertaking left to chance, a trip into the blue. It must end as it has begun, with conviction: Yes, may it be so!"[2]

So we close our precious Jesus Prayer, not with a casual "Over and out," but with a confident, "I am yours now, Lord, from this day forth and forevermore." When we can learn to say "Amen" as the ancients did, with all their heart, mind, soul, and strength, we will begin the lifelong journey of not merely saying but living this great prayer, a pilgrimage that will carry us through to the end. In that way the end really does become the beginning, the beginning of life for all of us.

Notes

Chapter 1: Pray Then like This

1. Emily Gwathmey and Suzanne Slesin, *On Earth as It Is in Heaven: The Lord's Prayer in Forty Languages* (New York: Penguin Books, 1994).
2. Everett Fullam with Bob Slosser, *Living the Lord's Prayer* (New York: Ballantine Books, 1980), p. 7.
3. Tertullian, *De oratione* 1.6 (Corpus Christianorum, Series Latina, Tertuliani, opera I), p. 258.
4. Daniel Migliore, ed., *The Lord's Prayer: Perspectives for Reclaiming Christian Prayer* (Grand Rapids: Wm. B. Eerdmans Publishing Co., 1999), p. 2.

Chapter 2: Our Father Who Art in Heaven

1. Eugene H. Peterson, *The Message: The Bible in Contemporary Language* (Colorado Springs, CO: NavPress, 2002), p. 1754.
2. Emmet Fox, *The Sermon on the Mount* (New York: Harper and Brothers, 1934), p. 161.
3. James Charlesworth, "Jewish Prayers in the Time of Jesus," in *The Lord's Prayer: Perspectives for Reclaiming Christian Prayer*, ed. Daniel Migliore (Grand Rapids: Wm. B. Eerdmans Publishing Co.), pp. 47–48.
4. William Barclay, *The Gospel of Matthew* (Philadelphia: Westminster Press, 1956), vol. 1, p. 203.
5. Oswald C. J. Hoffmann, *The Lord's Prayer* (San Francisco: Harper and Row, 1982), p. 16.
6. Pierre Raphael, *God behind Bars: A Prison Chaplain Reflects on the Lord's Prayer* (Mahwah, NJ: Paulist Press, 1999), p. 12.

Chapter 3: Hallowed Be Thy Name

1. Craig S. Keener, *Matthew* (Downers Grove, IL: InterVarsity Press, 1997), p. 142.

2. Olive Ann Burns, *Cold Sassy Tree* (New York: Bantam Doubleday Dell Publishing Group, Inc., 1984).
3. William H. Willimon, *Lord, Teach Us: The Lord's Prayer and the Christian Life* (Nashville: Abingdon Press, 1996), pp. 48–49.
4. Gerhard Ebeling, *On Prayer* (Philadelphia: Fortress Press, 1966), p. 57.
5. Jean-Pierre de Caussade, *The Sacrament of the Present Moment: Self-Abandonment to the Divine Providence*, trans. Kitty Muggeridge (San Francisco: Harper and Row, 1982). First published in France as *L'Abandon à la Providence divine* (Desclée, 1966).
6. Karl Barth, *Prayer* (Philadelphia: Westminster Press, 1952), pp. 42–43.
7. Jaroslav Pelikan, ed., *The Preaching of Augustine: "Our Lord's Sermon on the Mount"* (Philadelphia: Fortress Press, 1973), p. 111; Cyprian, "Treatises, On the Lord's Prayer," in *Ancient Christian Commentary on Scripture*, ed. Manlo Simonetti (Downers Grove, IL: InterVarsity Press, 2001), p. 132.
8. Helmut Thielicke, *Our Heavenly Father: Sermons on the Lord's Prayer*, trans. John W. Doberstein (Evanston, IL: Harper and Brothers, 1960), p. 43. Published in Germany under the title *Das Gebet das die Welt umspannt* (Stuttgart: Quell-Verlag, 1953).
9. Bette Greene, *Summer of My German Soldier* (New York: Puffin Books, Penguin Putnam Books for Young Readers, 1973).

Chapter 4: Thy Kingdom Come

1. Frederick Buechner, *Wishful Thinking: A Theological ABC* (New York: Harper and Row, 1973), p. 49.
2. Pierre Raphael, *God Behind Bars: A Prusib Chaplain Reflects on the Lord's Prayer* (Mahwah, NJ: Paulist Press, 1999), p. 47.
3. Karl Barth, *Prayer* (Philadelphia: Westminster Press, 1952), pp. 49–50.
4. Catherine Marshall, *A Man Called Peter* (New York: McGraw-Hill Book Co., 1951), p. 10.

Chapter 5: Thy Will Be Done

1. William H. Willimon, *Lord, Teach Us: The Lord's Prayer and the Christian Life* (Nashville: Abingdon Press, 1996), pp. 61–62.
2. John Claypool, *Tracks of a Fellow Straggler* (Harrisburg, PA: Morehouse Publishing, 2004); Harold S. Kushner, *When Bad Things Happen to Good People* (New York: Avon Books, 1981).
3. Willimon, *Lord, Teach Us*, p. 68.

Chapter 6: On Earth as It Is in Heaven

1. William Nichols, ed., *The Third Book of Words to Live By* (New York: Simon and Schuster, 1962), pp. 119–20.
2. Joachim Jeremias, *The Lord's Prayer* (Philadelphia: Fortress Press, 1964), p. 21.
3. Will Campbell, *God on Earth: The Lord's Prayer for Our Time* (New York: Crossroad, 1983), p. 34.

4. Karl Barth, *Prayer* (Philadelphia: Westminster Press, 1952), p. 54.
5. Bob Lively, *A Portrait of Prayer: Lessons for the Soul* (Georgetown, TX: WordWright.biz, 2003), p. 15.
6. William Sloane Coffin Jr., *Once to Every Man* (New York: Atheneum Publishers: 1977), p. 130.

Chapter 7: Give Us This Day Our Daily Bread

1. George Morrison, in *Classic Sermons on the Lord's Prayer*, ed. Warren Wiersbe (Grand Rapids: Kregel Publications, 2000), p.104.
2. Frederick Dale Bruner, *The Christbook* (Waco, TX: Word Books, 1987), p. 249.
3. William Barclay, *The Gospel of Matthew* (Philadelphia: Westminster Press, 1956), vol. 1, p. 219.

Chapter 8: Forgive Us Our Debts/Trespasses/Sins

1. Helmut Thielicke, *Our Heavenly Father: Sermons on the Lord's Prayer*, trans. John W. Doberstein (Evanston, IL: Harper and Brothers, 1960), p. 91. Published in Germany under the title *Das Gebet das die Welt umspannt* (Stuttgart: Quell-Verlag, 1953).
2. Everett Fullam with Bob Slosser, *Living the Lord's Prayer* (New York: Ballantine Books, 1980), p. 81.
3. Oswald C. J. Hoffmann, *The Lord's Prayer* (San Francisco: Harper and Row, 1982), pp. 55–56
4. Ernest T. Campbell, *Locked in a Room with Open Doors* (Waco, TX: Word Books, 1974), pp. 20–28.
5. Lance Morrow, "I Spoke . . . as a Brother," *Time* 123, no. 2 (January 9, 1984), p. 28.
6. Frederick Buechner, *Wishful Thinking: A Theological ABC* (New York: Harper and Row, 1993), pp. 28–29.
7. Gardiner Day, *The Lord's Prayer: An Interpretation* (Greenwich, CT: Seabury Press, 1954), p. 74.
8. Bob Lively, *A Portrait of Prayer: Lessons for the Soul* (Georgetown, TX: WordWright.biz, 2003), p. 18.
9. Pierre Raphael, *God behind Bars: A Prison Chaplain Reflects on the Lord's Prayer* (Mahwah, NJ: Paulist Press, 1999), p. 90.

Chapter 9: Lead Us Not into Temptation

1. Helmut Thielicke, *Our Heavenly Father: Sermons on the Lord's Prayer*, trans. John W. Doberstein (Evanston, IL: Harper and Brothers, 1960), pp. 119–20. Published in Germany under the title *Das Gebet das die Welt umspannt* (Stuttgart: Quell-Verlag, 1953).
2. Peter C. Whybrow, *American Mania: When More Is Not Enough* (New York: W.W. Norton and Co., 2005).
3. Oswald C. J. Hoffmann, *The Lord's Prayer* (New York: Ballantine Books, 1980), p. 69.
4. Thielicke, *Our Heavenly Father, p. 128.*

Chapter 10: Deliver Us from Evil

1. John Schwartz, "Longtime Expert on A.L.S. Now Knows It All Too Well," *New York Times*, sec. F, Feb. 22, 2005.
2. William Barclay, *The Gospel of Matthew* (Philadelphia: Westminster Press, 1956), vol. 1, p. 253.
3. Scott Peck, *The People of the Lie: The Hope for Healing Human Evil* (New York: Simon and Schuster, 1983).
4. William H. Willimon, *Lord, Teach Us: The Lord's Prayer and the Christian Life* (Nashville: Abingdon Press, 1996), p. 90.
5. Susan Nelson, "Deliver Us from Evil: Through the Eyes of Marian Kolodziej," *Installation Address as Directors' Bicentennial Professor of Theology and Culture* (Pittsburgh Theological Seminary), p. 8.
6. Gardiner Day, *The Lord's Prayer: An Interpretation* (Greenwich, CT: Seabury Press, 1954), p. 90.
7. Karl Barth, *Prayer* (Philadelphia: Westminster Press, 1952), p. 74.
8. Christian Smith with Melinda Lundquist Denton, *Soul Searching: The Religious and Spiritual Lives of American Teenagers* (Oxford and New York: Oxford University Press, 2005).
9. Rudolf Schnackenburg, *All Things Are Possible to Believers: Reflections on the Lord's Prayer and the Sermon on the Mount*, trans. James S. Currie (Louisville, KY: Westminster John Knox Press, 1995), p. 90.

Chapter 11: Thine Is the Kingdom

1. Gerhard Ebeling, *On Prayer: Nine Sermons* (Philadelphia: Fortress Press, 1966), pp. 133–35.
2. Joachim Jeremias, *The Lord's Prayer*, trans. John Reumann (Philadelphia: Fortress Press, 1976), p. 32; see also Adolf Schlatter, *Der Evangelist Matthaus* (Stuttgart: Calwer Vereinsbuchhandlung, 1963), p. 217.
3. Helmut Thielicke, trans. John W. Doberstein, *The Prayer That Spans The World* (Cambridge, England: James Clarke and Co., 1978), p. 152. Published in Germany under the title of *Das Gebet das die Welt umspannt* (Stuttgart: Quell-Verlag, 1953).

Chapter 12: Amen

1. James Mulholland, *Praying like Jesus: The Lord's Prayer in a Culture of Prosperity* (New York: HarperSanFrancisco, 2001), pp. 130–33.
2. Karl Barth, *Prayer* (Philadelphia: Westminster Press, 1952), p. 78.

Further Reading

Ebeling, Gerhard. *On Prayer: Nine Sermons*. Philadelphia: Fortress Press, 1966.

Gregory of Nyssa. "The Lord's Prayer." In *The Lord's Prayer, The Beatitudes*. Translated by Hilda C. Graef. Ancient Christian Writers, no. 18. New York: Newman Press, 1954.

Gwathmey, Emily, and Suzanne Slesin. *On Earth as It Is in Heaven: The Lord's Prayer in Forty Langauges*. New York and London: Viking Study Books, 1994.

Jeremias, Joachim. *The Lord's Prayer*. Translated by John Reumann. Philadelphia: Fortress Press, 1976.

Migliore, Daniel, ed. *The Lord's Prayer: Perspective for Reclaiming Christian Prayer*. Grand Rapids: Wm. B. Eerdmans Publishing Co., 1993.

Mulholland, James. *Praying like Jesus: The Lord's Prayer in a Culture of Prosperity*. New York: HarperSanFrancisco, 2001.

O'Neal, Debbie Trafton, Taia Morley, and Nancy Munger. *I Can Pray with Jesus: The Lord's Prayer for Children*. Minneapolis: Augsburg Fortress, 1997.

Pelikan, Jaroslav, ed. *The Preaching of Augustine*. Translated by Francine Cardman. Philadelphia: Fortress Press, 1973.

Raphael, Pierre. *God Behind Bars: A Prison Chaplain Reflects on the Lord's Prayer*. Mahwah, NJ: Paulist Press, 1999.

Schnackenburg, Rudolf. *All Things Are Possible to Believers: Reflections on the Lord's Prayer and the Sermon on the Mount*. Translated by James S. Currie. Louisville, KY: Westminster John Knox Press, 1995.

Shoemaker, Stephen. *Finding Jesus in His Prayers*. Nashville: Abingdon Press, 2004.

Wiersbe, Warren, ed. *Classic Sermons on the Lord's Prayer*. Grand Rapids: Kregel Publications, 2000.